A Little, Brown Book

First published in Great Britain in 2002 by
Little, Brown, an imprint of Time Warner Books UK

Based on the transcript of an interview by Mary McCartney Donald, directed by Alistair Donald. Recorded on 13/14 February 2001 at House of the Redeemer, New York.

Design: Norman Hathaway and Donat Raetzo
Design production: Lindha Eriksson and Gerard Rada Nedich
Additional photo research Zoë Norfolk

Thanks to Lilian Marshall, Zoë Norfolk, Lisa Power and Robby Montgomery

ISBN 0-316-86032-8

Printed in the United Kingdom by Butler & Tanner Ltd

Little, Brown
an imprint of Time Warner Books UK
Brettenham House
Lancaster Place
London WC2E 7EN

www.TimeWarnerBooks.co.uk

WINGSPAN

Text from interviews with
Paul McCartney
Text edited by Mark Lewisohn

Art direction Norman Hathaway

Contents

Facing page: Watched over by Martha and photographed by Linda, Paul McCartney picks out the notes for a new song, *Two of Us*, late 1968

Wings was always a difficult idea. In the Beatles, we had always said that any group having to follow our success would have a hard job. With Wings, I found myself in that very position.

However, it was a choice between going on or finishing, and I loved music too much to think of stopping. So eventually Linda and I had the idea of forming a simple little band that would allow us to continue making music.

At first – having known the great achievements of the Beatles – it was quite a struggle. Everything we did seemed to be measured against them, so even if we had successes they felt sometimes like relative failures. I realise now that we did amazingly well to keep our heads above water and keep going. As this book shows, we eventually won through, made some cool music, enjoyed great times and had fans who, to this day, remember Wings with more affection than even the Beatles.

Looking back, I'm surprised to realise that we did ok. In fact, I think some of the stuff was good and I'm very proud we had the courage to prove that what we had set out to do could be done successfully.

This book tells the story.
Paul McCartney

A decisive moment in the Beatles' ending is captured by the lens of Linda McCartney. It is September 1969 and all but George convene at the Apple office in Savile Row, London, for a business meeting. Paul suggests the Beatles try to bury their differences by reinvesting in the band and returning to live performances. John announces instead that he wants 'a divorce'.

Left to right: John Eastman (Linda's brother and Paul's business adviser), Paul, John, Yoko, Allen Klein (Apple's business manager; John, George and Ringo's ally), Ringo, Ringo's wife Maureen, and Allen Klein's colleague Peter Howard

The Beatles had a meeting to sign a new deal with Capitol Records. We were sitting around in this rather tense atmosphere and I was saying `I think we should go back on the road, go back to our roots. We should just go out and play together.´ And John looked me in the eye and said, `I think you´re mad.´

I met Linda in May 1967 in a club called the Bag O' Nails. It was my regular haunt after I'd finished working. She was over in London to shoot some photos and had gone down there with Eric Burdon and the Animals, friends of mine. I was in my normal alcove and they were just over to the left, and playing that night was Georgie Fame and the Blue Flames, one of the good bands. And I just looked over, saw her and there was an immediate attraction. So I did what I didn't normally do – I stood up and said, 'Oh, hi, my name's Paul, what's yours?' Then I had to say something else, so I said, 'We're going on to another club, would you like to join us?' We went on to the Speakeasy and heard *A Whiter Shade of Pale* for the first time. It became 'our song', because we heard it together that night.

Linda met John, George and Ringo at a party at Brian Epstein's house, when we launched *Sgt Pepper*. It was another good, casual meeting between Linda and me, and again we were attracted to each other, but it wasn't like we were going to stay together forever and forever. It was only later, when she kept coming back to my mind, that I realised she was great. I knew a lot of other girls and they just didn't seem quite as good.

At a certain age you start to think, 'I've got to get serious, I can't just be a playboy all my life.' And whenever I did, Linda came into my mind. So

eventually I thought that we should spend more time together, to see if we really were attracted or if it was only a casual thing. We were making the *White Album* at the time and I said, 'Do you fancy coming over to London and staying a little bit longer? You could stay with me.'

Linda came over to England from America. The Beatles were at Abbey Road that night, recording *Happiness is a Warm Gun*. She'd got her flight and gone straight to the house, so I left the session and went home – it was just around the corner. And that began a period of our living together and getting to know one another. Our backgrounds were dissimilar – she was from New York and I was from Liverpool – but as we got to know

each other we realised we had many things in common: rock and roll, nature, art, photography, painting …

I've now learned about 'quality of life' – how to live, how to feed yourself – but back then I was just a guy in a band, often on tour or in hotels or restaurants, and I never had to fend for myself. Before Linda came over to England, to live with 'a Beatle', she imagined that I led an aristocratic lifestyle! We used to laugh about it afterwards, 'Your royal carriage awaits you …'

My fridge had half a bottle of sour milk and a little bit of dried cheese. Linda took the mickey out of me for that. The house was a bit of a tip, really, just a place to sleep, but when she arrived it became a place to *live in*. At one point, slightly later in our relationship but still during that period, Linda said to me, 'I could make you a nice home.'

At a certain age you start to think, 'I've got to get serious, I can't just be a playboy all my life.' And whenever I did, Linda came into my mind.

That really moved me, because I was a great home-lover, and having lost my mum at fourteen I really missed all that. Linda was very good to be with because she'd say things like, 'Let's get out of London.' I'd say, 'OK, where do you want to go?' and she'd reply, 'Let's just go and get *lost*.' I particularly remember one morning after a late-night recording session, and here I was – unshaven, scruffy, really knackered – going out with a girl. I apologised and she just turned to me and said, 'It's allowed.' I liked that. Those were really good *balancing* times for me. Sometimes I brought a guitar along; I wrote *Two of Us* about Linda and me, heading out for nowhere.

Linda and her daughter Heather had an apartment at 83rd and Lexington, the tenth floor. I'd always liked New York but never lived there – I'd just stayed in hotels, running to a limo. I'd never done

much walking, which is one of the fun things about New York, or catching a cab and going around the park or the Village. We went on the subway, to 125th Street I think, and walked to the Apollo. Nobody knew who I was, or her; it was away from all the fame and I could be totally free.

Linda Eastman photographed by Paul McCartney, winter 1969–69

Another Paul McCartney photo: Linda and Heather on Manhattan, late 1968

I wrote *Maybe I'm Amazed* in my
early days with Linda. I was sitting
in London, playing my piano,
and the song kind of wrote itself
– reflecting my feelings towards her.
It's remained a favourite of mine.

A quiet stroll in Central Park, snapped by Paul

One of the earliest Linda Eastman
photos of her husband-to-be, taken
at Kennedy Airport in May 1968.
Paul and John had been in New York
to announce the formation of
the Beatles' company Apple Corps

John, George and Ringo weren't at
the wedding, which might have been
because of the tensions of the time,
or because we decided to do it quickly.
It seems like an important point now
but it wasn't at the time – it was just
the two of us wanting to get married
quietly. My dad wasn't there either
– I'm not sure he was pleased with me
about that, but my best excuse was
that it was the spirit of the times. We
didn't want a big fuss.

The New York City snowscape, taken by
Linda Eastman during the home visit with her new
English boyfriend

It was a fun little wedding. We giggled our way through it.

It was a fun little wedding. We giggled our way through it. It was quiet when we got to the registry office but word must have got out because it seemed like there were millions of people around when we came out, hanging out of office windows and cheering. I just made sure that I stayed near Linda, and kept shouting, 'She's with me, she's the bride!' Heather was with us too.

When it came to Linda being in the public eye, maybe once or twice we thought, 'This is going to be hard,' but I don't think we ever thought of giving it up. Linda wasn't prepared for the bitchiness, though. Some journalists were uptight about my marrying an American divorcee with a child. They made up that she was 'the Eastman Kodak heiress', and one of the comments was 'Paul's landed on his feet'. But when people bad-mouthed us it made us even more determined to prove them wrong. It was a battle in some ways, one that we were determined to win.

My fans used to write on the wall outside the house, and to say that what they wrote about Linda was not complimentary would be the understatement of the year. I owed it to Linda to give her some quality of life, so one day I went out and said to the fans, 'Look, I have just got married, and I'm going to be trying to bring up a family. I'll do an autograph but that's it. The old days are over.' It was hard to get rid of them but one evening I snapped and they saw a side of me which I hadn't shown them until then. That did the trick.

The Beatles had a meeting to sign a new deal with Capitol Records. We were sitting around in this rather tense atmosphere and I was saying to the guys, 'I think we should go back on the road, go back to our roots.

We've got too crazy, we should just go out and play together.' And John looked me in the eye and said, 'I think you're mad. And I wasn't going to tell you until after we've signed the Capitol deal, but I'm leaving the group.' Our jaws dropped but he was excited by it, it was an adrenaline rush for him. He was controlling the moment. He said, 'It's like getting a divorce.'

There was really no point in sitting around in London, getting involved in all the Apple dramas. When I look back, it obviously wasn't the most stable time of my life. I went crazy for a good few weeks – it was more than a lost weekend – and started to have one drink too many. It was the nearest I'd ever been to feeling insecure, paranoid, out of work, useless. Why bother to get up in the morning? But in the depths of my despair Linda was there to say, 'It'll be all right, you'll get out of this.' She talked me through it. If I'd have been on my own I'm not sure I would have survived.

On his way home – a Linda Eastman image of John Lennon at Kennedy Airport, at the end of his and Paul's visit to New York, May 1968

Recording in low profile – Paul at home in London, working the four-track tape machine used to capture the *McCartney* sounds

It was an intense time, but luckily I still had my music. **When you're going through the worst of times** it's good for your soul if **you can still make music.**

It was at this point that we thought, 'Let's just get away from it all' and went up to Scotland. I just had to get out into the mountains and the mist. We lived off our savings for a bit. There was no furniture on the farm so I built a bed for us, basically a mattress on some old potato boxes, we threw things together and lived very funkily. It was a time for rebuilding, literally – the house, the home and then finally the music ... once again.

recording. It was a good take, so we left it in. I made the whole *McCartney* album like that, and when I needed to go further we used a little studio in Willesden called Morgan, just to get a bit more high-tech. But I played all the instruments and we did a few harmonies together. It was funky, and still sounds good to me.

I really had to ask myself, 'Do I want to give up music, or keep going?' I got a four-track Studer recording machine, like the Beatles used for *Sgt Pepper*, put it in the corner of the living-room at my house in London and tried a very simple technique of just plugging directly into the back, not going through a mixing desk. It's a cool way to record because it's pure. If, say, I was doing a drum track, I'd play the drums, record it with one microphone, listen to it back, move the mike a little if there wasn't enough hi-hat or cymbal, and then re-record. Then I'd add bass by plugging the mike into track two and overdubbing while listening to track one through headphones. I'd do that with all with four tracks. It was very hands-on, primitive way of working. In the opening track, *The Lovely Linda*, you can hear the door squeak as Linda came in while I was

An early Scotland morn

Some of the songs on *McCartney* I had tried with the Beatles and they hadn't worked out. There was one called *Teddy Boy* – the unsuccessful Beatles version is on *Anthology*. The Beatles were breaking up and nobody had any patience, whereas in the earlier days we might have said, 'Why don't we try it like this?' So I thought, 'Right, I'll do it on my own album.'

Beatles breakup time – Paul consumes al fresco in his London garden

For the *McCartney* cover artwork we had a big wad of photos that Linda had taken, and the only one that wasn't of me with a guitar was a photo with Mary, our new baby, inside my jacket. I used to carry her that way to keep her warm. Eventually, we had so many photos that we couldn't see the woods for the trees, so we sent a pile of them to a friend – David Putnam, now Lord Putnam. He has a very good eye for an image and he called back and said, 'There's only one cover in this lot – the one with the baby in the jacket.' Just to be difficult, though, we put that on the back cover and put a photo of cherries on the front.

Apple was no longer a happy place: there was a lot of tension in the air. I rang Neil Aspinall – who was and still is the head of Apple – and said, 'Can I have a release date for this album I'm making?' He gave me one and I worked towards that. Then, suddenly, a letter came from the other Beatles, who were now with [manager] Allen Klein, which said that they were releasing *Let it Be* [the film and album] and were going to delay my album. I said, 'Wait a minute, I've made all my plans, I've got it all worked out …' We had another argument over that, which increased the tension even more. The word 'heavy' was coined during this time. I really did feel physically weighed down by it all, having such a bad time and, worst of all, feeling artistically constricted.

For business reasons, we had agreed to keep quiet about the Beatles' split, but after a while I was going crazy with the hurt and the disappointment of it all, the sorrow of losing this great band, these great friends. I thought it was unfair not telling people, so I broke the news in a press release for the *McCartney* album. Not being in the greatest frame of mind, I was dreading the press asking me, 'Are the Beatles happy?' I didn't want to lie through my teeth. So I announced in a press release that the Beatles had broken up. In actual fact, the breakup had happened months before, and it was John who did it. But it doesn't matter who broke the Beatles up – the Beatles were ready to break up. We'd come full circle and now we had to get on to something new, all of us.

It was an intense time, but luckily I still had my music. When you're going through the worst of times it's good for your soul if you can still make music.

Linda and I called it our 'funky period'. With the fame of the Beatles, everything was done for us. Like, around Christmas I'd ring up the office and say, 'Can I have a Christmas tree?' I had become used to having everything done for me, and hadn't realised it. A lot of people who find fame and money like to leave humdrum things behind. When Linda and I got together she said, 'Let's go and pick out our own Christmas tree' and 'Let's go down to the shops and buy something for dinner.' I like all those things, they're ordinary, and important to me. So we started to put them back into our life and do things for ourselves.

We were on holiday in France and thinking about making another album. I'd written a few new songs and we thought that for a change we'd go to New York to record. It's a good place, with a lot of great musicians and would give us a different slant. We'd tried the amateur bit with *McCartney*, going back to square one; now we wanted to get a bit more professional. So we took the ocean liner *Ile de France* and sailed from Southampton over to New York.

Linda and I called it our 'funky period'.

It was a crazy journey. I wore shades a lot of the time and nobody really bothered us. But there was one woman who got annoyed at me coming into the dining-room wearing them. I thought, 'What the hell. I'm on holiday, I'll do what I want' and I didn't particularly want to have to relate to some of these people. She got annoyed, saying, 'Take your sunglasses off. Elizabeth Taylor is on this boat and she doesn't wear them.' I said, 'Well I'm not Elizabeth Taylor!'

When we got to New York we started
to audition musicians. I put the
word out via a couple of people and
some drummers came by to play.
Denny Seiwell, who had been working
as a session man, was the best.
He's a nice guy and we got on well, so
we started the *Ram* sessions with
him. I also auditioned guitar players,
playing a couple of songs together
to see if I liked their personality, if we
got along. Dave Spinoza and
Hugh McCracken emerged from
those auditions, really good guys.

The British sense of humour, which
can be a bit sarcastic, almost got
me into trouble after one guitar
audition. The player was a little bit
serious and as he was leaving he
said, 'ok man, See ya. Peace and love.'
And I said, 'Yeah, war and hate.'
His face dropped — it was like I was
the devil. I had to run after him saying,
'It's a joke!' He forgave me, I think.

I like the idea of writing songs about ordinary people and day-to-day lives, and *Another Day* is one of them. We all get up in the morning and do our usual stuff, yet somehow – even through it all – there are often magic moments. We recorded it in New York with the help of Phil Ramone and it was a hit – which, at that time, was especially pleasing.

I had an uncle – Albert Kendall – who was a lot of fun, and when I came to write *Uncle Albert / Admiral Halsey* it was loosely about addressing that older generation, half thinking 'What would they think of the way my generation does things?' That's why I wrote the line 'We're so sorry, Uncle Albert'. There's an imaginary element in many of my songs – to me, Admiral Halsey is symbolic of authority and therefore not to be taken too seriously. We recorded it in New York and George Martin helped me with the orchestral arrangement. I was surprised when it became a big hit.

Back in Scotland, I had a four-track recording studio installed at the farm, which we called Rude Studio, so I was able to demo and experiment and make bits and pieces of music. Eventually, when we started to put a band together, we could rehearse there.

'Have drums, will travel'
– Denny Seiwell
on arrival in Scotland

Recording *Ram*

Having had such a good time making a few *Ram* tracks in New York we went out to LA as well, because there were a couple of guys there I wanted to work with. It was great weather and we rented a house on the beach, on Ocean Park Boulevard. While we were in LA we started to put together the album artwork. Rather than get a smart studio photo and design, we did it ourselves – we took some prints and made a collage with glue, grass out of the garden, a little bit of hair, some felt-tip drawings, and so on. For the front we used a Scotland picture of me, holding a ram. It was a little bit unusual, but it worked.

I was happy with *Ram* as an album, though it didn't get very good reviews. Because we were still in the shadow of the Beatles everything we did was compared to them. We also bought into that, but – looking back – it actually did very well.

The *Ram* artwork takes shape

Shot for the camera: take one. The Rude boys –
and girl – band together for the first time. Scotland
in the summer of '71 and the new combo, not yet
named, takes shape

I didn't really want to keep going as a solo artist, just me and a guitar, so it became obvious that I had to get a band together.

Johnny Cash had just come back, and he had a band and was touring.

Linda and I talked it through and it was like, 'Yeah, but let's not put together a supergroup, let's go back to square one.'

I didn't want to ring up famous mates – Eric Clapton and Ginger Baker, that kind of thing – and suggest forming a band. That didn't seem right. I don't know why.

I'd only ever really been in one group – the Quarry Men which became the Silver Beatles and then the Beatles – and that was John's group which I'd joined. Now I was putting together a group for myself. It was quite a challenge, and good fun. Going back to basics made it difficult but it seemed the only way to do it.

My much-publicised rivalry with John Lennon during the Ram period came about from the business problems we were experiencing after the breakup of the Beatles and the temporary end of our company, Apple. I had tried hard to save everything in the battles that ensued and I think there were one or two people on John's side who stirred things up and encouraged the rivalry. I've certainly heard some interesting stories since, but John and I had a love for each other that managed to survive through it all, and we ended up close friends.

With *Ram* we'd enjoyed the experience of working with other people. But to be in a band with complete strangers is a bit of a shock. With the Beatles, John, George and I had played together for quite a while before we became successful. But the thought of working with complete strangers used to terrify me – the idea that you're sitting there, look to one side and think 'Who the hell's that?' So having my best mate, my wife, in the new band, was to be very comforting.

Denny Seiwell, American drummer, wonders what he's got himself into

With *Ram* we'd enjoyed the experience of working with other people. But to be in a band with complete strangers is a bit of a shock.

Denny Laine – retired Diplomat and Moody Blue loses Balls, finds Wings

Crude Rude jam

P: Do you think you can handle being in a band?
L: *I don't know. I've never done it before.*
P: But when the Beatles started we'd never done it before, either. Can you imagine: we're standing behind a curtain, the curtain opens, there's people there... How would you feel about that? Would it completely freak you or, could you get into it?
L: *I think I could get into it.*

That was how it started. I said, 'Right, let's try it, we'll put a band together.'

I had always admired the way he sang *Go Now*. I knew he was a good singer, and a nice guy, so we asked him if he wanted to be in a band with us and he said yes.

From the *Ram* sessions, Denny Seiwell seemed like a good band member and we also asked Hugh McCracken if he wanted to join. He came to Scotland and rehearsed with us but he didn't like the idea of it. I think he was happier in New York. We were starting from the ground up. So Hugh bowed out. That was OK – I understood why.

Wings-to-be – Linda is still heavily pregnant –
get to work inside the Scottish stone shack. Young
Heather McCartney auditions as guitarist

Wings in the woods – an outtake from the
Wild Life cover shoot

I wanted another male to sing along with and remembered Denny Laine, whom I'd known from his days with the Moody Blues. They once toured with the Beatles and we'd had some good laughs. I had always admired the way he sang *Go Now*. I knew he was a good singer, and a nice guy, so we asked him if he wanted to be in a band with us and he said yes. With me on bass, Linda on keyboard, Denny Seiwell on drums and Denny Laine on guitar, that became the first line-up of the band.

During our early days Linda and I wrote songs together. It was a combination of things. Being so close, we naturally gave each other ideas. Also, the song publishing company refused to recognise her as a writer, which I thought was a bit of a cheek.

Our first album was recorded in just two weeks. I'd read that Bob Dylan had just made a quick album, and I really liked the idea, because we tended to take longer and longer to make records. The early albums by the Beatles hadn't taken long and it seemed to me that Dylan was getting back to that. I was a great admirer of his – and still am to this day – so I thought, 'Well, if it's good enough for him, let's do it.' So I got the band together and said that we should make it quickly, doing it almost live.

Linda was heavily pregnant with Stella while we were recording the band's first album. The family thing was already intertwining: we were starting a family and we were making an album. If she'd have wanted to stop the sessions we would have done, but it just didn't arise. A lot of women work until two weeks before the baby is due and that's what Linda did. Even though it was a rock band, it was still a job.

I used to check out the other Beatles' solo albums, and I think they checked out mine, too. There was a strange competitiveness now that we were separated. It was odd to have feelings of jealousy for each other after having been so tight for so long ...

All this time, we still didn't have a name for the band. When Linda gave birth to Stella there was a complication: something called placenta previa. She had to have a Caesarian and stay in hospital to recover. To be supportive, I stayed there with her, sleeping in a little camp-bed. It had been such

So Wings became the name. And the first album became *Wings Wild Life*.

a touch-and-go thing, such a drama, that I was imagining angels' wings. And I thought, 'That's a nice image – WINGS. I wonder if there's been a band called Wings?' That's how the name came about, in King's College Hospital, in London, as we recovered from the birth of Stella.

A press launch is always a good excuse to have a night out, so we invited friends and journalists, played the album, danced and had a few funny people come on to entertain. I wore an outrageous big check suit that I thought would be good. When I went to collect it from the tailor that morning he

told me that it wasn't finished. I said, 'Maybe not, but it's a look!' So I went to the party with the cotton and the stitching showing, and everyone said, 'Your suit's not finished.' I said, 'Yeah, I know. Great, huh?'

'There's middle-C and here's the chord of C.'

We were up in Scotland and I was painting the big corrugated-iron roof. During that time, Linda had bought some of the first reggae records that hit Britain, *Tighten Up*, and she'd play them downstairs while I was painting the roof. We both loved the music and going to Jamaica became our big ambition. When we did, we really fell in love with it: the country, the people, the music, the lifestyle, the weather. We spent weeks there, soaking up a lot of reggae – it was the start of rap but they used to call it toasting. There was a radio station called RJR that played reggae all day long, and a little shop in Montego Bay called Tony's Record Store where we used to sift through all the 45s. It reminded us of the 1950s. We'd buy them by the titles – one record was called *Poison Pressure* by Lennon-McCartney. I thought, 'Oh yeah? This is interesting.' It was no song I'd ever had a part in, nor John. Maybe we weren't the only Lennon-McCartney in the world, though – perhaps it was Moses Lennon and Winston McCartney.

It had been such a touch-and-go thing, such a drama, that I was imagining angels' wings. And I thought, 'That's a nice image – WINGS.'

Major Beatles fan Elton John, just becoming a superstar himself, meets one of his heroes at the Wings launch party

Birth of a baby – Stella McCartney – and the band name Wings

Because of all the business troubles at Apple we really didn't have much money. Well, I had some but I couldn't get at it because it was frozen. But Linda had some savings from her photography so we were able to live on that for a while. We always used to say that if all the money went, if we became broke, then we'd go to Jamaica and live in a little shack.

After our first visit to Jamaica, Linda wrote her first song, *Seaside Woman*. We cut a demo and I played drums. I didn't have a snare drum, though, so I used a couple of ropes. Again, that's why we called it our

'funky period' – it was all improvised. The harmonies on tracks like *Seaside Woman* became central to Wings. That sound was slightly different to what anyone else was doing. Elton John said he really loved our harmonies, and when I later worked with Michael Jackson he asked for Linda to be on the harmonies. Our voices did blend very well together.

Because of all the business troubles at Apple we really didn't have much money. Well, I had some but I couldn't get at it because it was frozen.

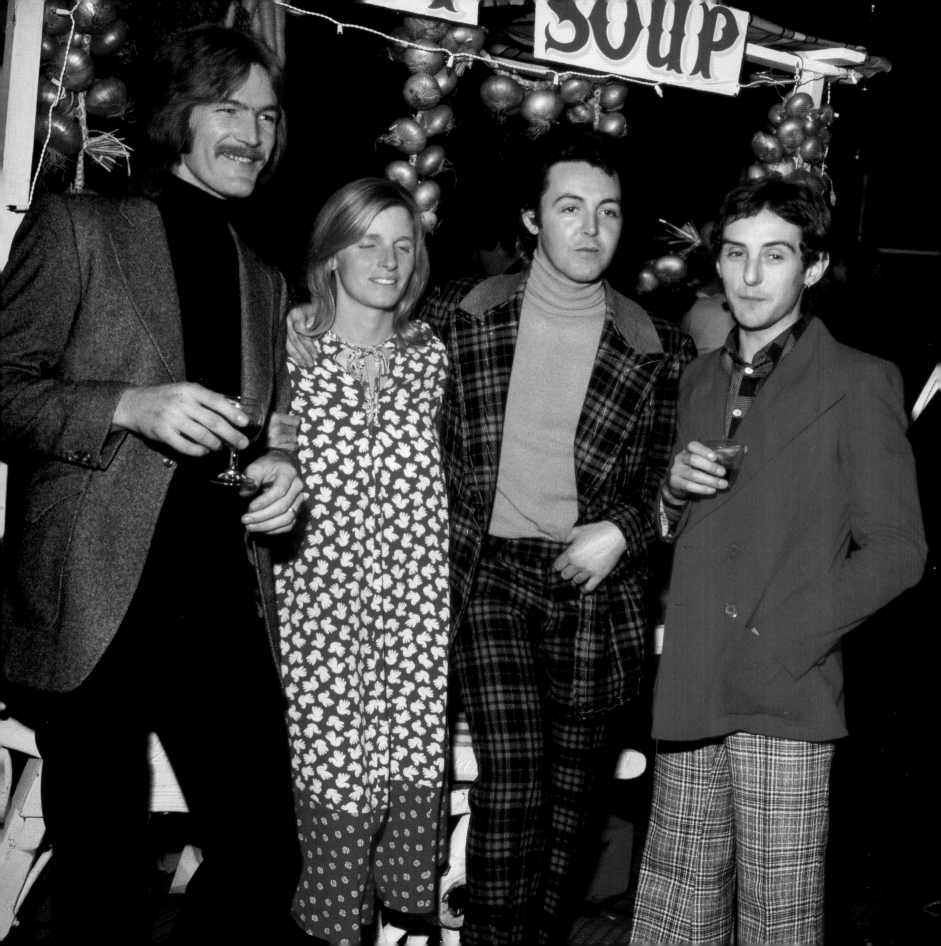

London, February 1972, and a new rock combo is ready to roll, destination ... who knows where?

After the ICA rehearsal we went out on the university tour. Being a new band we had to practice and this seemed like the best way to do it. It was a fairly crazy way to do it actually, but – let's put it this way – we got to know each other. We had some hilarious moments.

Our roadies happened to know Henry McCullough, who had been in Joe Cocker's Grease Band. They said he was really good so we invited him along to a rehearsal and we all got along well. He became Wings' lead guitarist, and so now we had a complete five-piece band ready to rock.

We found a place in London called the ICA – the Institute of Contemporary Arts – where artists could practice, and there was a cafe so we could get lunch. I liked the place, and it allowed bands to rehearse. We went in and started working on some new songs. I'd just written one called *The Mess* so we rehearsed that. Above all, we tried to get the band together.

Give Ireland Back to the Irish was written after Bloody Sunday. British soldiers had fired at a crowd of demonstrators and there were deaths. From our point of view, looking at it on the TV news, it was the first time people questioned what we were doing in Ireland. It was so shocking. I wasn't really into protest songs – John had done that – but this time I felt that I had to write something, to use my art to protest. I wrote *Give Ireland Back to the Irish*, we recorded it and I was promptly phoned by the chairman of EMI, Sir Joseph Lockwood, explaining that they wouldn't release it. He thought it was too inflammatory. I told him

that I felt strongly about it and that they had to release it, and he said, 'Well, it'll be banned.' And of course it was – the BBC could not play it. But it was number one in Ireland, and in Spain for some reason. It was just one of those things you have to do in life, because you believe in the cause. And protest was in the context of the times.

I wasn't really into protest songs – John had done that – but this time I felt that I had to write something, to use my art to protest.

I knew *Give Ireland Back to the Irish* wasn't an easy route, but it just seemed to me to be the time. I had to say something. All of us in Wings felt the same about it. But Henry McCullough's brother, who lived in Northern Ireland, was beaten up because of it. The thugs found out that Henry was in Wings.

Henry, the two Dennys, Paul and Linda: Wings from left to right, rehearsing at the ICA, London, February 1972. They were about to record debut single *Give Ireland Back To The Irish* and head out on the road to promote it

We had decided that we would go back to square one. We wouldn't book a big tour, we wouldn't even book hotels, we'd just go in a van – the band, the kids, the dogs – take off up the motorway and find somewhere to play. We wanted to play at universities, where there was a captive audience, and our idea was to go in and say, 'Do you want us to play for you?' It was as simple and as mad as that.

Our roadie would go in, find someone from the Students' Union and say, 'I've got Paul McCartney in the van, with his band Wings. Do you want 'em to play for you?' 'Yeah, sure, pull the other one.'
'No, really. Come and see.'
The student would come out to the van and I'd say, 'Hello, yes, it's me. We'll play for you if you want.'

We didn't have many songs. To be precise, we had eleven, which – at about three minutes a song – is a 33 minute act. They wanted longer so we repeated things. 'We've had a request to do *Lucille*. We did it earlier but now we're gonna do it again for Jenny Babford on the science course.' Whatever. We just repeated things, especially our new single *Give Ireland Back to the Irish*. The gigs went quite well but it's funny to look back and realise that we had such little material.

The Students' Union in Newcastle had booked the City Hall, which was quite a big gig – a few thousand people. It wasn't big by today's standards perhaps, but it was big for us then. We went to play *Wild Life* and I said, 'Ah one–two–three...' Nothing. Just silence. I looked around at Linda and she mouthed to me, 'I've forgotten the chords.' By this time the audience was starting to giggle, thinking we were doing a comedy routine. So I walked over to the keyboard and when I got there I also couldn't remember the bloody chords. By this time the audience were rolling with laughter. Then suddenly Linda remembered them and we went into the song, our hearts beating fast. There were quite a few moments like that. That was the problem of going back to square one – you've got to go through the baptism of fire. Eventually we got a bit better, started to actually know our songs and even perform more than eleven of them.

The university tour was really a public practice. The Beatles made all their mistakes in private, at the little clubs

Eventually we got a bit better, started to actually know our songs and even perform more than eleven of them.

before we were watched by any critics. With Wings, I knew that when we went public all the critics would be sitting there with their sharpened pencils – 'Oh, he's not as good as he was.' It was like I had returned to amateur status, trying to relearn the whole game.

The rock photographer as rock star; Linda and her mean tambourine

Before certain gigs Linda would suddenly think, 'God, what have I got myself into here?' From being a photographer she was suddenly in a band with me. Crazy.

The Beatles were old and comfortable gloves – you just slipped them on and hey, it all happened. Wings was new gloves – you had to break them in. Before certain gigs Linda would suddenly think, 'God, what have I got myself into here?' From being a photographer she was suddenly in a band with me. Crazy.

Linda was pretty confident most of the time, but sometimes there would be a nail-biting moment. Everyone gets nervous and I knew she'd have to go through that – that's the reality of being in a band. But she conquered those nerves, got on with it and was really gutsy. By the later Wings tours she was the ballsiest one in the band, with no apparent nerves whatsoever.

I taught Linda the basics of the keyboard. 'There's middle-C and here's the chord of C, now get on with it!' She took a couple of lessons and learned some bluesy things. Eventually she had a lot of work to do – songs like *Live and Let Die* have quite complicated chords. But she did very well and made it look easier than it was.

The critics would say, 'She's not really playing' or 'Look at her – she's playing with one finger.' But what they didn't know was that sometimes she was playing a thing called a Mini-Moog, which could only be played with one finger. It was monophonic. You can use as many fingers as you want but there's only one of them going to work. She rode through all those storms; it didn't really bother her.

Linda got on very well with everyone in the band, although there were some tense moments because she wasn't as adept musically as they were. They had studied music or at least played for a long time and she was saying, 'Wait a minute, let me get this right ...', which led to one or two tense moments.

We thought we were in it for fun. This was music, not nuclear science. The world didn't depend on it, it was just something we wanted to do, so if we got it wrong – big deal. We didn't have to justify ourselves. The good thing about music is that if people don't like it they don't have to buy it. If they do buy it, great, that's the validation.

We got invited on a lot of TV shows, particularly the two of us together, as if we had to justify what we were doing, but we thought, 'Why should we? It's our life.' We didn't have to explain ourselves to anybody. And we were both so resolute that once we started a thing we were determined to finish it. Particularly when the critics kicked in and said we were rubbish – it made us more determined, it became a 'We'll show you!'

Summer holiday, 1972-style. Cutting a multicoloured dash through Europe, Wings shake some dust off this old bus, as they traverse continental byways in search of sound stages.

We knew we were going to tour in Europe, and that the weather would be nice, and the idea of being stuck in a bus all the time, going from city to city, hotel to hotel, wasn't too appealing. Not much quality of life there. So we decided to travel around in an open-top bus. We put mattresses on the top deck and got some sunshine as we travelled from one place to another. And we painted the outside psychedelic, like a magic bus.

If you look at it very straight, very conventionally, it was a quite mad thing to do, to put a playpen on the top deck of the bus and put all the children in there while driving around Europe. It was not what you'd expect from a normal band. But we weren't a normal band.

In the early days of Wings I wouldn't play Beatles songs. People would shout 'Sing *Yesterday*!' but I wouldn't do it. I didn't want to rely on all the old props because we were trying to build a new audience, not satisfy people who liked the Beatles and might have been coming to see us just for nostalgia's sake. We were trying for a new, young following, which eventually we got. But it took a while, and we had to fight a lot of prejudices to do it.

that was done afterwards. But there was a little period in the 1970s where it seemed like a cool thing to do and we did it. It was like growing up, but I know we didn't play so well if we were drunk.

times it was equated with pot, and so, again, the BBC banned it. They played the other side, *C Moon*. That was a safer track, a nice track, but *Hi Hi Hi* used to go down better at concerts.

For me, part of the thrill of Wings was that it was like getting on a tightrope. It was challenging. After a while we had to work out what the heck we'd bitten off, and how we were going to manage. There were a few nerve-racking moments.

People would say, 'What's he doing with his old lady up there?' Wives normally stay in the background and there she was, with me on stage. Now it's quite common to have all-girl bands, or bands with a girl in it, and it doesn't look the least unusual. At that time, it did look odd.

The drug scene was less harmful than it was going to get. Shortly after this period people were doing much harder drugs, and you were seeing casualties. Looking back on it, I realise we were lucky to get through it.

For me, now that I'd got this great relationship with Linda I didn't want to go off touring around the world and just say 'See ya in a few weeks, babe!'

Quite a few bands around at that time were into drinking, and though it's not really my thing, Wings got snared

into that for a while at the beginning. With the Beatles I'd never drunk before going on stage – anything like

Busted in Gothenburg – Paul and Linda are jailed for five hours and given an instant fine for possessing cannabis; August 1972, during Wings' first European tour

Hi Hi Hi was a song of the times. As anyone knows about that period, drugs were fairly widespread. Looking back on it now I have a completely different perspective, but at the time it seemed to us that everyone was doing it. To me, *Hi Hi Hi* was a perfectly harmless little rock and roll song – 'we're gonna get high-high-high'. In my mind, if someone gets drunk then they're getting high. But because of the

People would say 'What's he doing with his old lady up there?'

Three-fifths of Wings, children, roadies, dog and muddy football – a spot of sporty bonding, 1972

Anybody who's been in a band will tell you that it's quite a tricky thing to accomplish. You've got to blend all the personalities in a kind of marriage. It's not easy with any group of people, but doing it the particular way we did, with me having been in this other rather famous band, was especially difficult.

As a songwriter it was always one of my ambitions to compose a James Bond film song. I realised it wouldn't be easy but it appealed to me. Ron Kass, who had worked at Apple, knew the people at the film company and he asked if I would be interested in writing the theme for *Live and Let Die*. I said

yes, and they agreed. They sent
me the Ian Fleming novel and I read
and liked it, and the next day I sat
down to see if I could write the song.
I got the fairly straightforward
idea of 'live and let die, and live and
let live', and I also knew that I had
to incorporate explosions. George
Martin produced the session and
wrote an arrangement for the middle,
and Linda wrote the reggae bit. We
recorded it with an orchestra and
then George took it out to wherever
they were filming, in the Caribbean
somewhere. The producers listened
to it and said, 'That's a great demo,
who's going to make the real record?'
George had to tell them this was
the real record. They had thought I
was going to write it for someone
else to sing.

The cook of the bus – Linda in the galley as the tour
continues its romp around Europe

Raising kids isn't easy, as any parent
knows. It's a lovely thing to do,
but the last thing anyone would say
is that it's easy. So combining that with being in a band,
also not an easy thing to do, was
difficult. But we loved it. It was what
we wanted to do.

I had earned my living from being a musician since I was
seventeen so I didn't really know much else. But
combining it with raising a family was tricky. The children had to be educated
and we had to take tutors with us on tour. They all

turned out smart, though, so it must have worked. People would say to us, 'Oh, you're dragging your kids around the world – Australia, Japan, America – it's bad for them.' And we'd say, 'No, it's a geography lesson ...'

It wasn't always fun. There were difficult times, especially if any of the children were ill. And it would be a strain on our relationship. But, what isn't a strain on a relationship? I don't think there's any such thing as an ideal couple who breeze through life never having arguments and whose children never get ill. Life's not like that. But at least we were doing what we wanted to do.

I have to own up:
I've not had a conventional life.

We'd be rehearsing and then have to stop to change a nappy.

My Love was inspired by Linda. We'd been together a while and were having a great time, and as I sat down at a piano to follow the muse I was thinking about Linda and the song came. It was nice to be able to say, 'Here, I've written this one for you.'

Musical chairs, Wings style; Abbey Road Studios, 1972

We had an interesting moment on the *My Love* session.
Instead of piecing it together and overdubbing I wanted
to record it live with an orchestra. Everyone was ready
in Abbey Road studio two, we knew exactly what we
would be doing, and then just before the take Henry
came over and whispered in my ear, 'Do you mind if I try

something different on the solo?' I had to make one of those decisions — to stick with what we'd rehearsed or to run with his new idea. At the risk of messing the thing up I went with his idea and he pulled a great new solo out of left field. He really rose to the occasion.

My Love crossed over into the black audience, which I liked because I've always admired black music so much.

My Love was always a very popular song in the live act. I'd see couples putting their arms around each other, which I always thought was a nice romantic moment.

Henry McCullough, guitar virtuoso and early 1970s rock star

Rock colleagues and soul mates – Paul and Linda
nestle down on the tour bus.

Paul McCartney inside the EMI studio in Lagos.
All of the photos in the forthcoming pages are from
Linda's new Polaroid camera

I thought Lagos was going to be gorgeous but I'd overlooked the realities of going to somewhere like that — the studio wasn't built properly and it was like monsoon season. Again, though, out of adversity came something good.

The studio was interesting. We wanted vocal booths – isolation booths – but the people didn't quite know what these were.

I'd written a lot of our next album and felt I had some nice songs, and I was looking around for somewhere exciting to record. I asked EMI, our record company, for a list of all the studios they had around the world. We usually worked at Abbey Road and I knew they had a studio in Germany. It turned out they also had one in Rio and, I think, China, and they had one in Lagos, Nigeria. Being a fan of African music I thought it would be cool to record there. Linda, Denny Laine and I were up for the idea, but Denny Seiwell and Henry, it turned out, were not.

A band is a democracy. Everyone gets a say and you've all got to agree on things. One person can say, 'No, I'd like to do it like this,' and one person can lead it, but, basically, people have to be happy for a band to work. It's

like any sports team or group of actors – they've got to feel good about each other for it to work.

We were due to fly out to Africa on a Saturday, but – the night before – Denny and Henry phoned and said, 'We're not coming ... and we're leaving the band.' At first it seemed like a tragedy for Wings but then I turned it around. Out of that tension I was determined to do the best album we'd made. The next day, as planned, we went to Lagos, but just the three of us – without a drummer and lead guitarist.

I thought Lagos was going to be gorgeous but I'd overlooked the realities of going to somewhere like that – the studio wasn't built properly and it was like monsoon season. Again, though, out of adversity came something good.

The studio was interesting. We wanted vocal booths – isolation booths – but the people didn't quite know what these were; so we drew pictures, explaining how booths are made of wood and glass, and they made them for us.

The children of Lagos

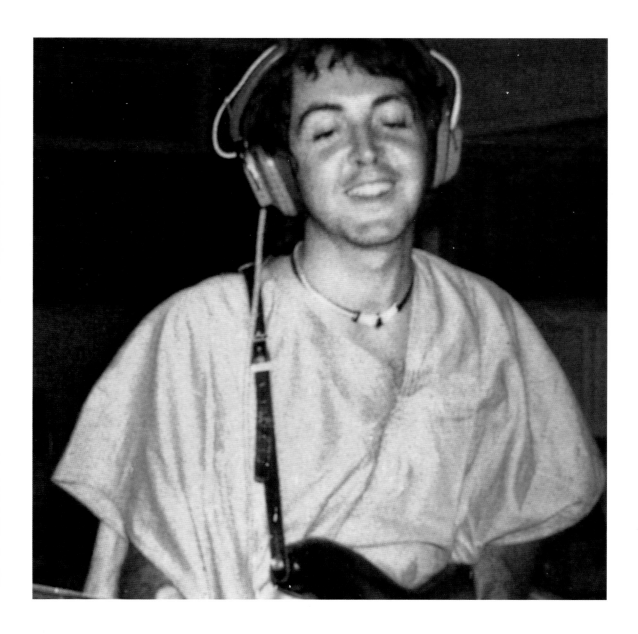

Laying down *Band on the Run*

Linda was screaming, 'Leave him alone, he's a musician!'

It was so exciting to be in Africa – the music, the culture.

People who lived there told us that under no circumstances were we to walk on our own – we must drive everywhere – because it wasn't safe. So, of course, we thought, 'What do they know? We'll do what we want...' After spending one particular evening at a friend's house we decided to walk back to our place. It wasn't too far, about half an hour away, and we knew the route.

As we were walking along, carrying a cassette recorder and cameras, a car pulled up, a guy wound down the window and offered us a lift. I have an innocent attitude – like, we're all friends, we're all brothers – so I thought, 'What a nice guy!', thanked him and said we were happy to walk. The car drove off, went about twenty yards and then stopped again, and as we walked alongside the doors opened and five guys jumped out, holding knives.

I'm going, 'What do you want? Cameras? Take 'em. Tape recorder? Take it. Money? Here!' Linda was screaming, 'Leave him alone, he's a musician!' Then they jumped back into the car, slammed the doors, and vroom, it roared off.

It was only then that we started shaking. We got back to our place about half an hour later and there was an immediate power cut. In our screaming paranoia we thought the robbers had followed us. We got into bed, pulled the covers up and went to sleep, hoping we'd wake up the next morning.

They took the cassettes I was carrying, which had demos of the new songs.

We carried on making the album but the stress caught up with me because a couple of days later I began to feel a bit odd and then fainted. Linda thought I had died. She had a point – when I came around even I was convinced I was going to die. We got a cab to the hospital where the doctor said I had been smoking too much and suffered a bronchial spasm.

Next day we went to the studio, still crazed from it all, and were told how lucky we were not to have been murdered. Apparently, we weren't killed because we were white – the muggers must have reckoned that we wouldn't be able to identify their faces. If we'd have been black they probably would have killed us. As it was, they took the cassettes I was carrying, which had demos of the new songs. Luckily, I remembered them. We joked later that they might have recorded over them, thinking 'Let's get some decent music on here.'

The top local musician, Fela Ransome-Kuti, who performed amazing live shows with his thirty wives dancing in topless grass skirts, showed up at the studio one day and accused me of being a Westerner out to steal black music. It could have been quite dangerous because he was a powerful local figure. So I played him our recordings and said, 'Tell me if you think I'm stealing your music. If you think I am then I won't use that track.' I knew we'd be all right – we hadn't gone there to steal the local rhythms, we had gone there because we thought it would be a cool place to record. He calmed down once he heard the tracks.

'Tell me if you think I'm stealing your music. If you think I am then I won't use that track.'

Paul confers with local musicians in EMI's Lagos studio, including Fela Ransome-Kuti (on Paul's left). Their suspicion that he had come to Nigeria to 'steal local rhythms' was unfounded but added to the steadily building tension prevalent during the *Band on the Run* recordings

In among all these horror stories there were some really good moments, and we had a lot of fun. People say that adversity and tension can make something better – that if you really have to sweat then the end-result is often sort of enhanced. *Band on the Run* certainly proved it. It was Wings' best album and won a Grammy.

On one of our Jamaican holidays we had heard that Dustin Hoffman and Steve McQueen were around, shooting the film *Papillon*. We were invited to visit the set and Dustin asked us back to his house for dinner. He was asking me how I write songs; I explained that I just make them up. He said, 'Can you make up a song

Mr Laine – suddenly Wings' lone Denny – cutting a
Fender guitar track for *Band on the Run* ...

about anything?' I wasn't sure, but he pulled out a copy of *Time*, pointed to an article and said, 'Could you write a song about this?' It was a quote from Picasso, from the last night of his life. Apparently, he had said to his friends, 'Drink to me, drink to my health, you know I can't drink anymore,' and then gone to bed and died in his sleep. So I picked up a guitar, started to strum and sing 'Drink to me, drink to my health …', and Dustin was shouting to his wife, 'He's doing it! He's doing it! Come and listen!' It's something that comes naturally to me but he was blown away by it. And that song became *Picasso's Last Words*.

Flying in the breeze ... handwritten lyric for *Bluebird,* one of the standout songs on *Band on the Run*

Shooting the *Band on the Run* cover at Osterley House, west London, October 1973, with a few well-known characters gathered to depict the title song's prison breakout.

Top left, Paul with TV presenter Michael Parkinson and his children. Top centre, actors James Coburn and Christopher Lee. Top right, some of the team before the photo shoot – Britain's champion boxer John Conteh is on Lee's left.

Middle left, singer and comic-actor Kenny Lynch. Middle centre, James Coburn with the cook, bon viveur and politician Clement Freud.

Bottom centre and right, out by the wall.

A song like *Let Me Roll It* came about by playing around with a little riff; if I'm lucky the rest of the song just comes to me.

Mrs Vandebilt was a good one. I didn't know anything about her but I just knew she was like … a rich person.

When we got back to England I saw a letter from EMI that said, 'Cancel your trip to Lagos – there has been an outbreak of cholera.'

After *Band on the Run* we had to address the fact that Wings was just me, Linda and Denny again, so we did our usual thing of holding drum auditions, this time in a London theatre. We saw a lot of guys, from which we picked Geoff Britton – a good, solid rock and roll drummer who also happened to be a major karate expert. And then I

The guitarist was a whizzkid named Jimmy McCulloch. He was still young, I liked him, we asked if he wanted to be in the band, he said yes.

remembered a great young guitarist who had played on a late–1960s record, *Something in the Air*, by a group called Thunderclap Newman. Pete Townshend had had something to do with it. It was a really cool record – it still sounds good today –

and the guitarist was a whizzkid named Jimmy McCulloch. He was still young, I liked him, we asked if he wanted to be in the band, he said yes.

Lead guitar in Wings switches from McCullough, Irish, to McCulloch, Scot.
Wee Jimmy celebrates his arrival in style. The band is about to enjoy its peak period

One cool dude, cruising Nashville in the summer of '74

So now it was me, Linda, Denny, Jimmy and Geoff, and with that line-up we took off for Nashville, to do some recording and get the band 'together'.

We stayed outside Nashville, in a place called Lebanon, at the house of the songwriter Curly Putnam – the writer of *Green Green Grass of Home*. We rented his place for a couple of weeks and rehearsed in the garage. It was a good space to work the band, and at the end of that period, once we had got everything together, we went into a studio in town and cut *Junior's Farm* and some other tracks.

Nashville is a Mecca for songwriters and, though I'm not particularly into country and western, I liked all the players and the studios there. I'd always wanted to visit the Grand Ole Opry and Johnny Cash took us around one day. I was amazed at seeing rows and rows of old, dead chewing-gum stuck under the wooden pews. That's the kind of thing that sticks in my mind.

Paul and Linda with their business aide Alan Crowder, quite the suave Nashville cat

Geoff Britton didn't stay too long with Wings. I don't really remember why now, except that perhaps he didn't quite fit. While we were looking around for a replacement, a horn player called Tony Dorsey said that he knew a drummer who was really good, a guy by the name of Joe English. We met Joe and he was very interesting — he could do a lot of rhythmic things and was a really nice guy.

So Joe joined Wings and we all
trooped off to New Orleans to record
our next album, *Venus and Mars*.
Marshall Sehorn and Allen Toussaint
had a great studio there, Seasaint,
and it was around Mardi Gras
time, too. The line-up now was me,
Linda, Denny, Jimmy and Joe,
which I always felt was the best of
Wings. I felt really comfortable
with that band.

I had written the *Venus and Mars*
songs in Jamaica – we were getting
around a bit in those days! – and had
the album pretty much mapped out.

Changes on the drum stool once again. Exit the
English-born Britton, enter the American-born
English

We took a couple of days off and enjoyed Mardi Gras. Linda and I dressed up as clowns, thinking that no one would recognise us, but people in the street said, 'Hi, Paul.' We were shouting at all the guys coming past on the floats, 'Throw us something, mister!' We got millions of beads.

We were big fans of the group the Meters, so while we were in New Orleans we went to one or two shows. The R&B scene there is great, with some fine musicians, so when we hired a riverboat and went on the bayou the Meters played for us. Included with the *Venus and Mars* album is a photograph of Linda with a top hat, taken that night.

Joe English did a lot of very good playing on *Venus and Mars*. Even though we didn't use the style of New Orleans on the album, it influenced the way we felt about the music and added to the spirit. Joe was sure to drum funkier in New Orleans than if he was in Lancashire.

We also cut a song called *My Carnival*. Carnival was in the air and we were picking up on the New Orleans thing, which is a very particular music, funky Cajun type thing. Someone came to the studio and filmed a little bit of it, and Professor Longhair saw it on TV. It was really a steal from his stuff but he liked it – he thought it was a tribute – so he came to the studio, which again was great because he was a hero.

Having recorded *Venus and Mars* we decided to do a Wings world tour, the biggest we'd done. Wings' three core members – me, Linda and Denny – had been getting better and better, and now, with Jimmy and Joe, it really seemed to be gelling. Jimmy was a cool guitar player. Henry had been, too, but Jimmy seemed a bit special. And Joe was the final ingredient. We were ready to hit the road.

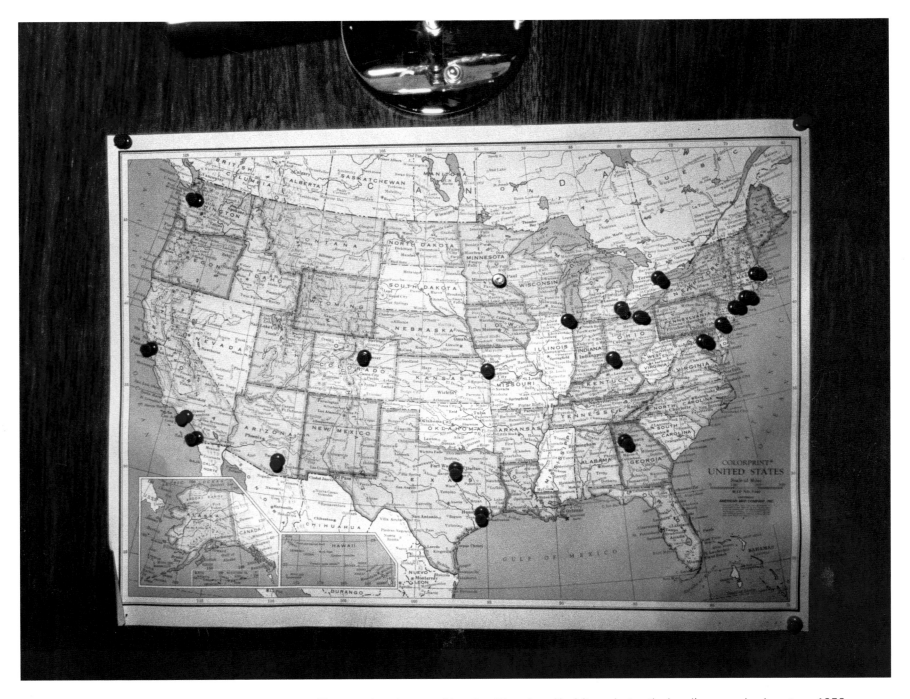

Pins over America – marking the cities played by Wings during the band's one and only us tour, 1976

After Britain, but before America:
Australia. A hugely successful tour Down Under

We'd come a long way and we were prepared. There were a couple of good songs on *Venus and Mars* and we wanted to promote it. Now was time for a big American tour – we put in a lot of rehearsal in London and assembled a stadium show.

Wings' finest tour of Britain, in autumn 1975,
was a huge success and fans everywhere gave them
a rapturous reception

Before we went to
America for the first time
we played another British
tour which was great
fun, and then we played
Australia and Europe

Of course, all it took was for one silly journalist to write, 'I hear that the Beatles could reunite on this tour' and the story spread like wildfire. So, in the first week or so of Wings' tour, the opening question in all the press conferences was, 'Paul, is it true that the Beatles are gonna show up and reunite?' In a way it was good, because it meant that everyone was going to buy a ticket, to see if it happened. But mostly we felt disappointed because it was detracting from what we had with Wings.

I always had to answer those questions about the Beatles reunion, so I came up with a Muhammad Ali-type verse:

The Beatles split in '69, and since then they've been doing fine.

If you ask that just once more, I think I'm gonna break your jaw.

Wings fans milling around outside
the Southampton Gaumont on the opening night
of the 1975–76 tour

One year later the tour returned to Britain for
the closing dates, at which this fetching piece of
voguish apparel could be purchased

Venice was a memorable concert. We bounced laser beams off the famous Venetian architecture. Zagreb was also great for me because the audience took over and sang *Yesterday* on their own and I let them do it. It was a very warm moment.

I said it each time and made sure
everyone knew this wasn't about a
Beatles reunion but a Wings tour.
It was like, 'Never mind the Beatles,
this is Wings, this is a good show
to see, this is something completely
different.'

Come the first night, when we
did a good show, the news people,
the media, started to accept it,
saying, 'Hey, who cares about the
Beatles? This is a good band ...'
That was what we had wanted to
achieve from the start. We weren't
trying to do much more than
that – as musicians you just want
to get a good band.

Four years after the frayed nerves of Wings'
impromptu university tour, Linda steps out into the
vast American arenas a confident rock star

Linda had got through those
nervous, early years and was really
on top of it by this point, playing
quite complicated keyboard parts.
She was really cooking, doing
the cheerleader bit with the audience,
singing harmonies and playing
keyboards. She was very sassy, Linda.
You can see it in the old interviews –
she was confident and enjoying
being in the band. She had answered
all her critics.

Wings greeting a legion of devoted fans outside the Seattle Kingdome.
Inside – well that was a whole other story ...

We even managed to fill out the Seattle Kingdome, breaking the attendance record for the biggest ever indoor gig, something like 67,000 people.

Denny Laine bangs the drum for *Let 'Em In* and America's 200th birthday celebrations

That inevitable (but always moving) lighter moment

It was a good period all round. Linda,
Denny and I had put in a lot of time
and effort and felt comfortable, and
with the addition of Joe and Jimmy,
and the work we'd all put in, by the
time we got out on that big '76
tour we established ourselves as a
separate entity from the Beatles. It
was the culmination of Wings, really.

WINGS
OVER AMERICA fill the world
with silly love songs! There ARE
No WORDS FOR OUR love for the
BAND ON the RUN
RAM ON
moon
HI
HI
HI
PAUL!

Los Angeles. Wings recruit a starry new bass guitarist ...

Laser lights and the horn section adorn *Soily*,
a staple of Wings' touring repertoire

I hadn't played live in America
for over a decade, and it was great
to be back. When I play in an
English-speaking country I feel a
little bit more at home than if
I'm playing elsewhere because I
don't have to think about how to
communicate. I just talk naturally
and so feel a bit more as one with
the audience.

It was quite a high-tech tour,
with lasers and light shows. When
you play those big stadiums you've
got to provide that or people say,
'I came to see you and you were like a
little pinpoint on the horizon.' So
we tried to build a good set, use
visual effects and make the sound
system as good as possible. We
had a horn section and made really
good music.

I'd seen lasers in James Bond films,
where they could cut people in half.
I first saw one in a rock concert
when I went to see Led Zeppelin at
Earls Court in London, and I remember
thinking, 'How brave is that Robert
Plant? He's standing right in front
of this thing and it could cut him clean
in half ...'

It was an epic tour. Wings' touring era had started with us piling into a van and driving up the motorway. Now it was an intricately planned major operation, with a crew and a convoy of huge trucks.

'*Sure* every cent goes to the artist'

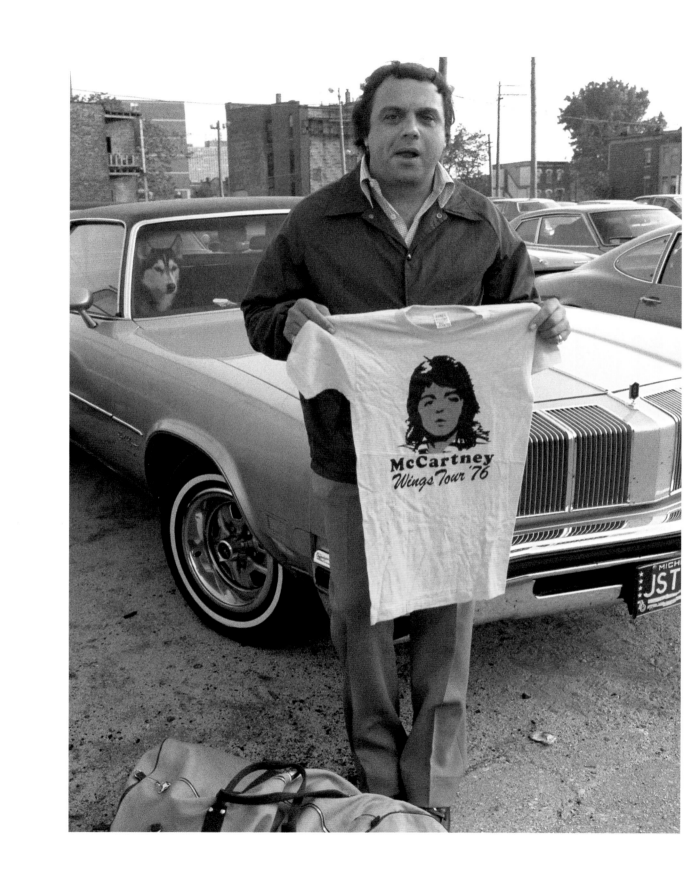

Pre-show transportation deluxe

Killing time on board the chartered
Wings Over America plane

Paul turns 34 and gets a special *Speed of Sound* cake

Jimmy McCulloch was a great player but he had an attitude. This is rock and roll – people do have attitudes; you can't expect everyone to be choirboys. But on one show on the Wings Over America tour – I think it was Boston – he refused to do the encore. Our thing was to run off, the crowd would ask for an encore, hopefully, and then we'd go back and do two more songs. So I was just running back for the encore when one of the roadies said, 'Jimmy's not coming on.' I ran down to the dressing room, grabbed him and gave him a rollicking – 'You're going back on – get on that stage now.' And he did, and played great.

The media said 'What are they doing, dragging their children around the world?'

Linda and I always had to consider the effect of these tours on the children, because we were taking them away from school. The teachers weren't always happy about it, but we hired tutors and encouraged them to find out what the children were learning at school and to continue the same work. Obviously it wasn't as good as them actually staying in school, but they all went on to do better academically than Linda and me.

We had decided our policy in the early days. We had children, we wanted to tour, what to do? We had long talks with teachers and other people about it, and the consensus seemed to be that we shouldn't remove them from school, that it would make life too unstable for them. Our reaction was, 'Yes, but what happens if we're in Australia and somebody rings up to say that one of the kids has a fever of 103 degrees?' Get back quick from Australia? So we just said, 'No, we're a close family, we've got to take them with us. Whether it's a good thing or not, we want to be with them.' We just felt that it was right.

When we had late-night parties we made sure the children were in bed first. This was very much against their will, I might add, but we played it pretty straight with them and they had as near to a normal life as possible in that sort of showbiz world. There are plenty other showbiz people who have brought up kids more conventionally, and they turned out to be nightmares.

The media said, 'What are they doing, dragging their children around the world?' as if we were taking them against their will. Well, let's just hope they brought up their kids better. I doubt it.

We had decided to send the children to state schools, and not pack them off to boarding schools. I came through the state system, and Linda and I figured that the best thing for our children would be to bring them up with their feet on the ground. You can bring children up in such a highfalutin way that they can never talk to ordinary people. We didn't want that. We figured that if ours wanted to get a bit sophisticated later in life then they could do that themselves.

It was a little bit unusual at the time, to take a family on a rock and roll tour. It had been groupies, sex and drugs, man. But because we were married it was no longer on the agenda. People can get a bit 'Hey, this is rock and roll, man, we're dangerous dudes, get out of my way, sucker' but I've never been into that. I think all that is phony.

Wings (and children) in the air, 1976, somewhere over America

It wasn't a heavy tour and it wasn't a really druggy tour. On some tours the band are heavily into drugs and it filters down to the crew. Our thing was always quite 'family' and the crew responded to our lead.

There were a few people who thought
it was a bit soppy, a Mums-and-Dads
tour, but it worked and there were
many more who thought, 'This is
interesting, they seem pretty normal.'
People often ask me how I stay so
normal and I just say, 'Well, I've
always been around normal people.'

Linda being there in Wings, to share
these great moments, was wonderful
for me. It was the payoff. This
crazy idea that we'd started in the
beginning, of 'What if you're up on stage with me?', had
actually worked. Even though it had seemed impossible,
that we'd never achieve it and she might never learn
all the music, it was all happening. It was really great for
me to be able to look over and see her there.

Linda loved horses so much, and one of her favorite breeds was the Appaloosa, a spotted horse bred by North American Indians. During that tour, while we were in Dallas, I used to drive to Fort Worth so that we could rehearse, and one day she spotted an Appaloosa away over in a field. We turned off the freeway and found the place, called Lucky Spot Stables.

Linda was saying to the man there, 'Could we look at that horse out in the field?' He said, 'I'm not selling him!' but Linda had fallen totally in love with the horse by this point. She rode him a little bit and – seeing this – the man realised she was a good horsewoman and eventually we persuaded him to sell. We named the horse Lucky Spot, took him back to England and started breeding Appaloosas.

When Linda was a child a lot of her friends were bought horses by their parents, and every Christmas morning she used to look out of her bedroom window and pray there would be a horse on the lawn, with a bow round its neck. But her father was never going to do that. It wasn't his thing. When we got married, and she told me all these stories, I thought, 'Right, I'm going to be the first person to buy her a horse.' She already had one named Cinnamon, and loved it, but when she saw Lucky Spot she was crazy for him.

And how's the ocean today, smooth or … ?

We were going to spend a month working quite intensively, so we wanted to have time off as well. It wasn't just work. We had another couple of boats for living on, taking a little dinghy across to the recording boat.

We thought of recording our next album, *London Town*, in the Virgin Islands – on the basis, I think, that it was warmer there. There wasn't a studio but we took mobile equipment and installed it on a boat – it was as good as being in a proper studio, but if you wanted to have a break you could dive off the side for a swim! It was the craziest decision, really, for an album called *London Town*, but this was a time when people were working like that. In the 1960s bands hadn't had the luxury of working that way, and now we had. We wanted to combine work and play.

We kept reasonable hours of recording. The Beatles worked late hours towards the end, but in our early days we recorded from like 10.30 in the morning until 5.30 in the afternoon. We tried to follow that, so in a typical day we'd swim, have breakfast, sunbathe a while, just like you do on holiday, and then putter across in the dinghy to the other boat and make some music for a few hours. Maybe if we really wanted to finish something we might go back to work after dinner, but normally we didn't.

Linda was pregnant with James at the
time but she didn't like to make much
fuss. She always took pregnancy in

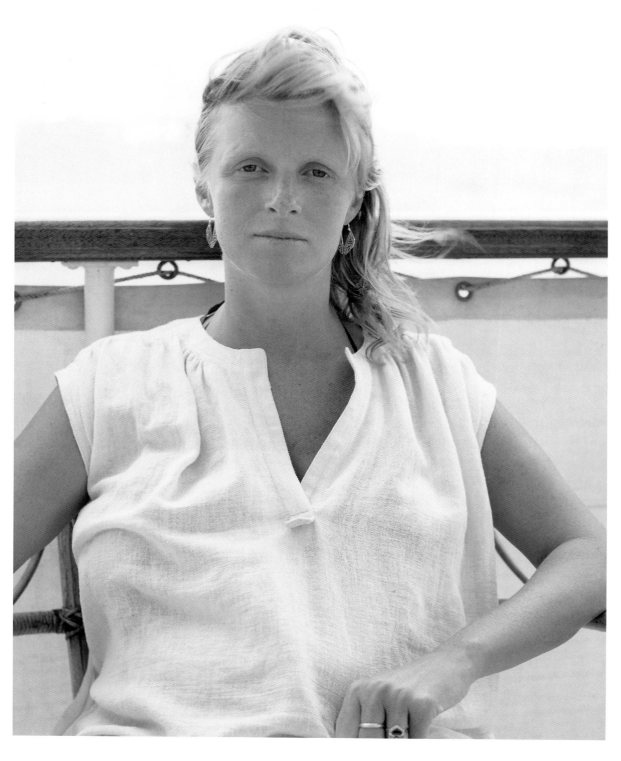

her stride. And recording is not like
playing live, trying to squeeze
into a stage dress – she only had to
sing and play.

We tried some mad things, like
standing on deck and playing a jam
while the engine was running. It was
silly and fun and I don't think it was
very good music. But the philosophy
was sound – if we have a good time,
it'll show in the music. *London Town*
ended up pretty good. I remember it
as an enjoyable period.

Three happy water Wings

We had a little flotilla, so we could
hang out with everyone, have parties
and so on, and then Linda and I
could go back to our own boat where
the children were. They were not into being tutored in a
holiday place like that, though. We wouldn't have
bothered with the tutoring if we'd thought it would be all right for them, but
you have 'parental responsibility'.

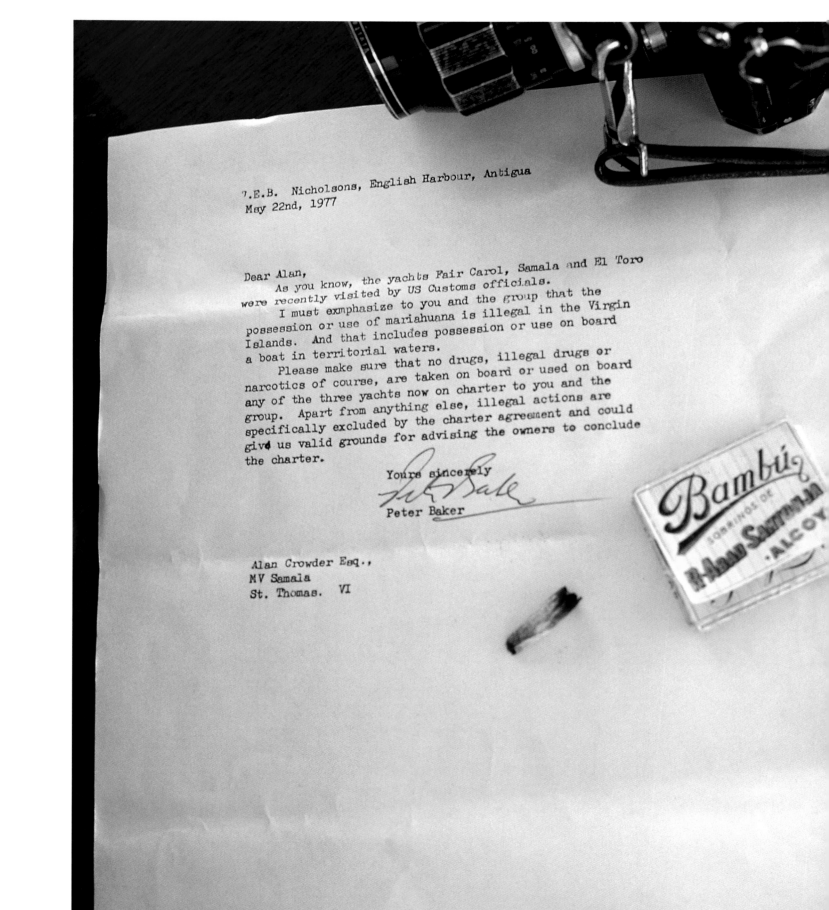

7.E.B. Nicholsons, English Harbour, Antigua
May 22nd, 1977

Dear Alan,
As you know, the yachts Fair Carol, Samala and El Toro were recently visited by US Customs officials.
I must exmphasize to you and the group that the possession or use of mariahuana is illegal in the Virgin Islands. And that includes possession or use on board a boat in territorial waters.
Please make sure that no drugs, illegal drugs or narcotics of course, are taken on board or used on board any of the three yachts now on charter to you and the group. Apart from anything else, illegal actions are specifically excluded by the charter agreement and could give us valid grounds for advising the owners to conclude the charter.

Yours sincerely

Peter Baker

Alan Crowder Esq.,
MV Samala
St. Thomas. VI

Jimmy stayed [with Wings] for a while but then I was rung up one morning by Steve Marriott, who used to be in the Small Faces and Humble Pie. A good singer, and he'd been a friend of mine. And he just said, 'Oh, hi, mate. Er, me and Jimmy have been up all night and he's decided he wants to leave your group and join mine.' I was a little bit put out but, well – what can you say to that? So I just said, 'Hey, good luck to you guys, I hope it works out,' knowing in my mind that it wouldn't, that they'd been up all night and had a great time but that this was not going to be a lasting thing.

Jim came on the phone and I said, 'Look, thanks a lot. See you around.' It didn't last … and, actually, Jimmy didn't last much longer himself. He died soon afterwards, of an overdose I think. He was always a little dangerous. As an older guy I did try and warn him a few times, like 'What's going to happen when you're thirty? You've got your whole life ahead of you.' But he liked partying too much and was getting into too many things. In the end, he was just too dangerous for his own good.

Naval attaché James McCulloch (RN)

In the 1960s, some accountant, one of our money advisers, said that I ought to find a good investment. There had never been much money in my family so I hadn't learned about it as a child – I thought the best thing was to stick it in the bank. So I said, 'All right, give me ideas then.' One day he rang and told me about a farm in Scotland. I said, 'No way do I want a farm in Scotland.' I had just gone from Liverpool to London, where the clubs are, where the scene is, where the music is, I didn't want to go to rural Scotland. But he kept going on about it, so in the end I agreed to have a look. I really didn't like it that much – there weren't any trees, just rolling hills – and I said 'Well, what's the good of this?' But he insisted so much that I finally relented and bought it.

To be honest, even after I went up there a couple of times I wasn't that keen on the place. It was an old hill farm, quite run down. My attitude about it only changed years later when Linda expressed an interest in seeing it.

I began to love being in Scotland. The children loved it, too – we could walk and they could run free

Linda loved the farm in Scotland. Her American view of the place was more romantic, more objective, than mine, and I could begin to see it through her eyes. She suggested we fix it up. How stupid was I not to have seen that? We turned it into a great place and suddenly I began to love being there. The children loved it, too – we could walk, seemingly forever, and they could run free.

It occurred to me that no great Scottish songs had been written for quite a while. I looked into it: all the bagpipe stuff was from the previous century and some of the popular folk songs were really old – and, I noticed, written by Englishmen. I wondered if I could write one, too – I certainly loved Scotland enough. So I came up with a song about where we were living, an area called Mull of Kintyre. It was a love song, really, about how I enjoy being there, and imagining I was travelling away and wanting to get back to it.

I did a demo in Rude Studio and worked out how the final version could include bagpipes. The bagpipe is an ethnic instrument from way back and I was aware that they can't play every note, so I invited the leader of the local pipe band to come to the farm. His name was Tony Wilson and he arrived with his bagpipes. We were sitting in the kitchen and I asked him to play me something while I tried to work out some guitar chords, and he said, 'We'd better go in the garden – the bagpipes are very loud.'

He started playing, and I could see that a lot of what he was playing was in the key of D. This meant that I could use A, and I worked out a scale that seemed to be all right. Actually, I didn't work it out quite well enough. When we made the record I got the pipe band to play the chorus; had I asked them to play the verse there was one note they couldn't have made.

Tony got the whole Campbeltown Pipe Band to rehearse the song and then they all came up to the farm, where we'd had a mobile studio installed in a barn. They came up in full dress, with kilts and sporrans. Some people hate bagpipes but I love them – I think they make a great sound, very soul-stirring. It was such a buzz for us because we hadn't worked with a pipe band before, and it was a buzz for them too, because it was something very different.

After we had recorded the best
take it was time to 'break out the ale'.
We were all becoming a bit rosy-
cheeked and some of the lads were
saying, 'Aye, that record'll be a
number one.' I wasn't sure, because
at that time the British music scene
was dominated by punk. I liked
punk – it was a breath of fresh air on

the scene – but releasing a Scottish waltz in the
middle of all that stuff was going to be unusual, to
say the least. As it happened, Heather was into
the punk thing, and I know that some of her friends
would go to the jukebox and put on *Mull of Kintyre*.

Mull of Kintyre was a screaming hit right across the board. It just went crazy. Alan [Crowder] at the office phoned to say it was selling 30,000 copies a day, which is a really good sale in Britain. As a joke I said, 'Don't ring me back until it's selling 100,000 a day.' Sure enough, a week later, it was selling 100,000 a day. Eventually it sold over two million, the biggest-selling single in Britain ever, bigger even than anything the Beatles had released. It stayed the biggest seller until the release of the Band Aid charity single a few years later. I was very surprised,

but then I remembered the session and all the wee Scots lads saying, 'Aye, that's a number one, that is.' They were right.

The success of *Mull of Kintyre* was strange, really. The song touched me – I liked it – but I wasn't sure it was everyone's cup of tea, and then it turned into the biggest seller of my career. In America, though, hardly anyone knows it. The US record company flipped the single and promoted the other side, *Girls' School.*

I've never released a record that I've not wanted to put out. In my case, the artist and the record company have to agree when releasing anything. I've been lucky in that respect – even in the very earliest days of the Beatles, when George Martin wanted us to issue a song he thought was a surefire hit, *How Do You Do It*, we didn't. We recorded it, but asked him not to release it, and he agreed.

Linda was heavily pregnant when we were recording *Mull of Kintyre*. When she was doing the harmonies someone at the session interpreted her having indigestion as a sign that she was going to produce a boy. This was great, because we'd had three girls and secretly wanted a boy. Later, she always loved the fact that when she was singing *Mull of Kintyre* James was 'there' with us.

The strangest thing happened about James's birth. I used to wear an old tweed coat which I picked up in an Oxfam charity-thrift shop. It was a really comfortable old coat and I wore it all the time Linda was pregnant. And toward the end of the pregnancy I found a blue baby-booty in the pocket. It was like a *Twilight Zone* moment.

Paul with sweet baby James

Linda was going to have the baby naturally and I was going to be present, but then at the last moment the doctor said she had to have another Caesarian. I waited outside, and a lovely black nurse came out and said, 'It's a boy!' I picked her up and hugged her, and then dashed to the phone to tell Heather, Mary and Stella.

Around the time of *London Town* Linda decided to renew her career as a photographer. I often used to say to her, 'I ruined your career, didn't I? You were Linda Eastman, respected photographer, got married to me and became "Mrs McCartney".' She'd been taking pictures throughout the previous few years but hadn't done anything with them, so she published a book [*Linda's Pictures*] and had an exhibition. It was the start of a reawakening of her career – eventually, she re-established herself as a great photographer.

The danger of spending all that time as a band member, wife and mother is that an important part of Linda's life was being forgotten. But I think her re-emergence as a photographer really only occurred because we'd established Wings and had a good degree of success, particularly with the '76 tour and *Mull of Kintyre*. It seemed like the right time for her to get back to her first love.

Wings was starting to become a bit more tense. Sometimes you sense when you've done what you set out to do. It happened with the Beatles – by the end we definitely felt 'That's it. Full circle.' After Wings' '76 tour I felt we'd really proved that we could make a band after the Beatles and be successful. As I say, *Mull of Kintyre* had sold more than any Beatles record in Britain. I got a sense of 'So what are we going to do, just keep on proving that we can do it? Or is it time for a change?' And, as it turned out, it was time for a change.

We had one band change in the Beatles, when we swapped Pete for Ringo. But, unlike in the Beatles, the guys in Wings were not my best mates or people I'd grown up with. They came and went for various reasons. Journalists used to have a bit of fun of it – 'Another band change for Wings,' kind of thing – but for us it was a case of 'if it has to be then it has to be'. If someone didn't seem to fit, or we thought we could do better, then we had to go with it.

After two action-packed years, from *Venus and Mars* to *Mull of Kintyre* by way of a world tour, Joe English heads back to America and Paul, Linda and Denny get that trio feeling once more

Wings was starting to become tense. Sometimes you sense when you've done what you set out to do

1978

Joe got homesick for America. He loved all the American home comforts and, as we know, there's plenty of them – when you live in America you get used to a certain way of life. He just came up to me one day and said, 'I really want to go back.' We could relate to that. I know that Linda was warned when she came over to live with me – her dad said to her, 'It rains all the time and all the guys are chinless,' but she'd been an Anglophile since she was young and was happier in England than the average American might be.

Wings Mk VIII, with drummer Steve Holly and lead guitarist Laurence Juber . Eschewing the studio once again, their sessions – for the album *Back to the Egg* and other tracks – took place in an assortment of buildings in remote parts of Kent, south-east of London

The calm before the storm: a rocking Christmas 1979. The Tokyo experience was just weeks away

No disrespect to them, but by the time we got Steve Holly and Laurence Juber in Wings I was getting a little bit fed up with 'yet another new line-up'. It was getting a

Getting very near the end. Wings take a break from their latest recording sessions

bit boring, to tell the truth – another dollar, another day, kind of thing. Even though they were good players, the whole Wings thing was becoming boring for me.

My enthusiasm had peaked, and Wings started to wind down. It's like someone with a career in sport – how many years can they keep winning gold medals? After a couple of years they're unlikely to have the same enthusiasm they had when they were really hungry for the first one. We were hungry with Wings right up until we proved our point, and then it subsided. Also, we'd settled a bit more into our home lifestyle and put down a few roots. All these factors came together and made me feel like … well, maybe I've had enough. I'd been in a band since I was fifteen or something.

When we planned to tour Japan everyone said, `Whatever you do, don't take any pot.´ And we said, `OK, OK, we won't.´ But we had been in New York and we had this pot and ...

Handcuffed and hauled away: Paul McCartney is arrested for possession of 219 grams of marijuana. A seven-year sentence hangs over his head.

The guy opens the suitcase and there, right on top … It's like a pop-up book – here, check this!

Well, to this day I have no idea what made me do it. I don't know if it was just arrogance or what. Maybe I thought that they wouldn't open my suitcase … I can't put myself back into that mindset now.

I could almost persuade myself I was framed. I don't think I was, but when you see the news footage – the guy opens the suitcase and there, right on top … It's like a pop-up book – here, check this!

It was the maddest thing in my life – to go into Japan, which has a seven-year hard labour penalty for pot, and be so free and easy. I put a bloody great bag of the stuff right on the top in my suitcase. Why didn't I even hide it in a pullover? I look at the footage now and I just think, 'That couldn't have been me.'

Another strange thing is, we hadn't really rehearsed enough. For the previous Wings tours we rehearsed a lot. It was almost as if I wanted to get *busted* – although I really didn't.

And suddenly I found myself in a Tokyo detention centre, not really knowing what had happened and in the midst of a very Japanese experience. 'Oh my God, what have I got myself into?' I was feeling really guilty about Linda and the children and the other guys. Like, 'I'm supposed to be a responsible father, what have I done?'

There are times in your life when you just think to yourself, 'You're an idiot.' This was one of them.

There was no VIP treatment here, I was just *busted*.

For the first three days I had headaches and nightmares, but after that I was actually getting quite a good night's sleep, learning a little Japanese and becoming friendly with the other guys, having a laugh.

It was like I was in a film. I was in handcuffs. Procedure was the word – we went through the whole procedure. There was no VIP treatment here, I was just *busted*. I had dropped myself right in it. I didn't know Japanese ways at all and didn't know about life in a cell.

I was in a little cell, on my own. Every morning a broom would be pushed inside; I soon got the idea – you had to brush the place out, tidy up your blankets and the little mattress they gave you, sit on it crossed-legged and call out 'Hai' or something. Then they would come along and let you out, and you could get washed. It took me a few days to get used to it, but then I tried to be the first one ready. I was like Steve McQueen in *The Great Escape* – except I didn't have the baseball to bounce.

I hadn't been separated from Linda since we'd got married. I realised that I had to keep my mind together, so I meditated a lot.

I wasn't allowed to see Linda for a few days but then a visit was arranged. It was just like the prison movies: I was behind a grille and we couldn't touch each other. It was all very alien. I just wanted news – 'Am I going to get out of here?' Linda said she didn't want to go home to England and leave me in Japan, that she would stick it out, a fact for which I was very grateful. I had visions of the children growing up in a little bungalow outside Tokyo, all speaking Japanese.

'What are you in for?'
'Marijuana.'
'Seven years.'

After the first visit Linda was allowed to return, and she could bring in a packed lunch for me. Breakfast in the morning wasn't exactly fattening: a little bread roll, a little bit of margarine, a sachet of jam and miso soup which, to this day, is not my favourite. People say, 'Hey, do you want a miso soup?' 'No, it's OK. I'll skip.' It reminds me of prison. Linda made me some really cool sandwiches, and, just like in a prison movie, she stuck a little love note inside.

I was hauled everywhere – into the car and across Tokyo to some judge's office. I was trying to look straight, like an ordinary good person. There's not a lot of understanding of British culture there and they asked me the weirdest questions. They said, 'You have MBE. What does this mean?' I told them it's Membership of the British Empire, an award that the Queen gives out, an honour. They said, 'Oh, you live at palace with Queen?' Well ... not exactly. I was tempted to say 'Yeah, and you'd better let me out of here before she finds out.' It would have been funny if it hadn't been so terrifying. I was facing a seven year stretch.

They had this thing they called the exercise period, which was actually the smoking period. Nobody exercised at all – you just walked in a line into another room and got out the cigarettes. I was the only Westerner in the jail. In Japan they have a mafia, and the mafia guys wear big tattoos; one of them was in the prison for murder when I was there. I was in with a few hard guys.

By this point I was starting to get a little sense of myself, just to keep my sanity, and so I would play games with the other prisoners. There was a left-wing guy who was in for social unrest – he spoke English so I could talk to him and communicate to the others. We would squat around a little tin, smoking and chatting; through the translator the big mafia guy says to me, 'What are you in for?' So I said, 'Marijuana.' The guy says, 'Seven years.' With my 'Steve McQueen' attitude I replied, 'No, no, ten!' which of course broke them all up.

We also learned to communicate through the wall. I couldn't speak any Japanese and – except for one – the other prisoners couldn't speak any English, but we communicated through brand names. I would shout 'Suzuki' and 'Honda' and they shot back, 'Magitatcha' – Maggie Thatcher – and Bell's, as in Bell's whisky. I'd hear them all applaud. You had to do something – or go mad.

One day one of the guys said, 'We know you are Western, and you would not want to take communal bath. We arrange a little room, bath and towel, you have private bath.' But – in for a penny, in for a pound – I said I'd join them. I didn't want to be 'the strange Westerner' off in some room on my own. The shower was very cold, but I was still 'Steve McQueen': us British, we can take it. From that I jumped into the hot tub with them all.

I was in there for nine days. When I came out, Linda said, 'You've become institutionalised.'

For two weeks after I got back I wrote it all down, the whole prison experience, kind of 'what I did on my holiday'. It's called *Japanese Jailbird* but I've never published it.

Sometimes I think I've had a sailor's life … touring the world, having mad experiences and bringing back souvenirs.

I could wish that Wings had found a very stable group of great players and stayed together until we decided we'd had enough, but it didn't work out that way. Life's not like that. You can dream, but things rarely work out exactly as planned. And in the end I think we just got fed up with having so many changes of personnel. That, and the fact that we had proved what we had set out to prove – which is that there was life after the Beatles.

I have no regrets about Wings. They were all good line-ups in their own way and we made good music with each of them. I look back now on the success and the tours and the chart positions, and – especially considering we were following the Beatles, which was virtually impossible – we did amazingly well.

One of the jokes I'd been waiting to use for the minute Wings split was to say 'Wings fold'! But, as it turned out, Wings didn't actually fold, they just sort of dissolved, like sugar in tea.

Paul McCartney/Wings discography, 1970–80

`I always wanted the name on the record label to be Wings, but the record company felt it would be more commercial for my name to be included. They said that people would go into a record shop looking for my name and therefore thought we ought to accommodate those people – so there were fluctuations from time to time – from Wings to Paul McCartney & Wings and back again.'

text by Mark Lewisohn

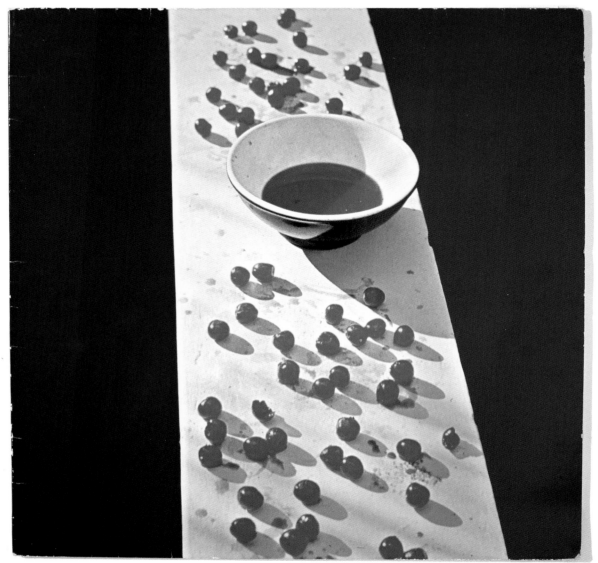

Maybe I'm Amazed
Words and Music by PAUL McCARTNEY

Northern Songs Limited

Recorded in secret at a time of strife and suspicion within the Beatles – when the final throes of the band met the last throws of the dice – *McCartney* was mostly home-made in St John's Wood, north London, microphone plugged straight into a four-track Studer tape recorder. (When eventually Paul ventured out to a couple of nearby studios he did so under a pseudonym and went unnoticed.) Speed was of the essence – the album was out within four months of its start – and the music was unpretentious: a mix of instrumentals, fully- and semi-developed ideas, noises-off and a freshness that was arresting. Tunes old – *Hot As Sun* was from before the Beatles, *Teddy Boy* was a track that hadn't made it on to *Let it Be* – sat comfortably alongside pieces new, including the outstanding *Maybe I'm Amazed*.

UK chart positions from *Music Week*
US chart positions from *Billboard*

McCartney
by Paul McCartney

April 17 1970 UK #2
April 20 1970 USA #1

produced by
Paul McCartney

The Lovely Linda
That Would Be Something
Valentine Day
Every Night
Hot As Sun
Glasses
Junk
Man We Was Lonely
Oo You
Momma Miss America
Teddy Boy
Singalong Junk
Maybe I'm Amazed
Kreen-Akrore

Ram
by Paul & Linda McCartney

May 28 1971 UK #1
May 17 1971 USA #2

produced by Paul & Linda McCartney

Too Many People
3 Legs
Ram On
Dear Boy
Uncle Albert/Admiral Halsey
Smile Away
Heart of the Country
Monkberry Moon Delight
Eat at Home
Long Haired Lady
Ram On
The Back Seat of My Car

Singles

**Another Day/
Oh Woman, Oh Why** *by Paul McCartney*

February 19 1971 UK #2
February 22 1971 USA #5

**Uncle Albert /Admiral Halsey/
Too Many People**

by Paul & Linda McCartney
August 2 1971 USA #1

**The Back Seat of My Car /
Heart of the Country**

by Paul & Linda McCartney
August 13 1971 UK #39

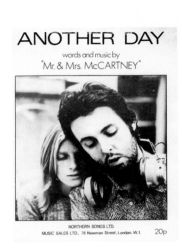

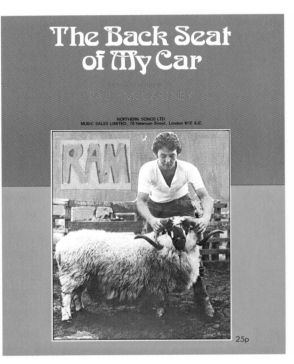

While *McCartney* had been a largely homespun affair, all Paul's own work save for Linda's occasional vocal support, *Ram* saw the couple working together more closely – the album was credited to Paul & Linda McCartney – and drawing upon a wider cast for significant production and musical support. The workplace this time was New York and Los Angeles and the sound was not pared back but lush, with strong orchestral arrangements. Musically, *Ram* is that typical McCartney mixture of rockers and ballads, epics and charmers, and the sum effect was aural attack, grooves swollen with sound. John Lennon believed he heard some personal criticism from his former partner among the lyrics, and he was right. Though recorded a year after the Beatles' breakup, bad vibes were still conspicuously public.

Wings Wild Life by *Wings*

December 3 1971 UK #11
December 6 1971 USA #10
produced by Paul McCartney

Mumbo
Bip Bop
Love Is Strange
Wild Life
Some People Never Know
I Am Your Singer
Tomorrow
Dear Friend

Singles

Give Ireland Back to the Irish /
Give Ireland Back to the Irish (Version)
February 25 1972 UK #16   by *Wings*
February 28 1972 USA #21

Mary Had a Little Lamb /
Little Woman Love by *Wings*
May 12 1972 UK #9
May 29 1972 USA #28

Hi Hi Hi / C Moon by *Wings*
December 1 1972 UK #5
December 4 1972 USA #10

The first album from a new band, *Wings Wild Life* was no real reflection of what was to come, its guiding ethos being Paul's intention to record the entire piece fast, much as Bob Dylan had recently cut his album *New Morning* in a week. *Wild Life* took two weeks to make, and at least one track – the opener, *Mumbo* – was a first-take recording. The McCartneys' fascination with reggae, which would bubble to the surface sporadically through the rest of the decade, was first illuminated here on the cover version of the old Mickey and Sylvia hit *Love is Strange*. The album displayed a sleevenote by one Clint Harrigan (later revealed to be Paul himself) and the sleeve itself purposely utilised the thicker cardboard prevalent on original 1950s albums; this was a theme echoed too in the running-order, Paul and Linda desiring 'fast numbers for dancing on one side, slow for necking on the other'.

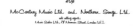

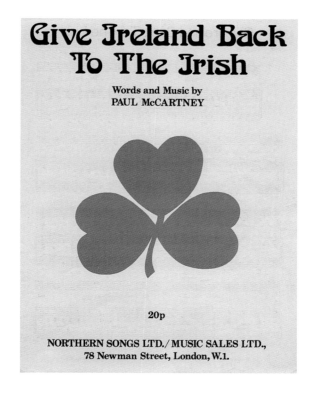

Red Rose Speedway

by *Paul McCartney & Wings*

May 4 1973 UK #5
April 30 1973 USA #1

produced by Paul McCartney

Big Barn Bed
My Love
Get on the Right Thing
One More Kiss
Little Lamb Dragonfly
Single Pigeon
When the Night
Loup (1st Indian On The Moon)
Medley: Hold Me Tight / Lazy Dynamite /
Hands of Love / Power Cut

Singles

My Love /
The Mess by *Paul McCartney & Wings*

March 23 1973 UK #9
April 9 1973 USA #1

Live and Let Die / I Lie Around by *Wings*

June 1 1973 UK #9
June 18 1973 USA #2

Now a five-piece, Wings plugged away at *Red Rose Speedway* through most of 1972, a year in which they issued no album (a first for Paul since the Beatles' debut) but three singles found decent success. By December there were enough tracks for a double-disc, ultimately halved. The undoubted standout was tender ballad *My Love* while the rocky tracks were designed for taking on the road: Wings' first British theatre tour coincided with the release. The album was packaged deluxe, including even a Braille message for Stevie Wonder, *We love you baby.*

Single

Helen Wheels / Country Dreamer

by *Paul McCartney & Wings*
October 26 1973 UK #12
November 12 1973 USA #10

Band on the Run

by *Paul McCartney & Wings*

December 7 1973 UK #1
December 3 1973 USA #1

produced by Paul McCartney

Band on the Run
Jet
Bluebird
Mrs Vandebilt
Let Me Roll It
Mamunia
No Words
Helen Wheels [not on ᴜᴋ album]
Picasso's Last Words (Drink to Me)
Nineteen Hundred and Eighty Five

Singles

Jet / Let Me Roll It by *Paul McCartney & Wings*

February 15 1974 UK #7
February 18 1974 USA #7

Band on the Run / Nineteen Hundred and Eighty Five by *Paul McCartney & Wings*

April 8 1974 USA #1

Singles

Band on the Run / Zoo Gang

by *Paul McCartney & Wings*
June 28 1974 UK #3

Junior's Farm / Sally G by *Paul McCartney & Wings*

October 25 1974 UK #16
November 4 1974 USA #3

Arriving three and a half years after the Beatles' final work, *Band on the Run* was already Paul McCartney's fifth album – and his third with Wings. Moreover, in the same period, the band also issued several singles not on those long-players, toured three times, shot a TV special and numerous videos and took a band holiday. All this while Paul and Linda were raising a young family. And yet of all these hectic projects *Band on the Run* is the one that really shouldn't have worked. Recorded in Lagos by a clipped Wings – Denny Seiwell and Henry McCullough departed on the eve of the trip – in an atmosphere that can best be summed up as intimidating, the collection is resolutely buoyant, with strong songs and confident musicality. Voted best album of 1973 by *Rolling Stone*, it became the best-selling album in Britain in 1974 and earned two Grammy Awards. Despite – or perhaps because of – the trials that surrounded its making, *Band on the Run* was a fine accomplishment and a statement that proves the old adage about art triumphing over adversity.

Venus and Mars by *Wings*

May 30 1975   UK   #1
May 27 1975   USA   #1
produced by Paul McCartney

Medley: Venus and Mars / Rock Show
Love in Song
You Gave Me the Answer
Magneto and Titanium Man
Letting Go
Venus and Mars (Reprise)
Spirits of Ancient Egypt
Medicine Jar
Call Me Back Again
Listen to What the Man Said
Treat Her Gently – Lonely Old People
Crossroads

Venus and Mars consolidated the success of *Band on the Run* and was the cornerstone of the 1975–76 world tour, ideal for taking on the road. The first of two collections featuring the band's most widely acclaimed lineup, with Jimmy McCulloch and Joe English as the latest recruits, it was recorded in New Orleans and Los Angeles. *Listen to What the Man Said* was a top-notch single, though buyers

Single
Listen to What the Man Said /
Love in Song by *Wings*
May 16 1975   UK   #6
May 26 1975   USA   #1

beyond the shores of Britain – and many of those within it, too – would have been puzzled by the inclusion of *Crossroads Theme*, the band's cover version of a low-brow TV soap opera signature. No matter, *Venus and Mars* soared to number one everywhere; in terms of sustained commercial success the album capped Wings' peak.

Singles

Letting Go (remix) /
You Gave Me the Answer by *Wings*
September 5 1975 UK #41
September 29 1975 USA #39

Venus and Mars / Rock Show /
Magneto and Titanium Man by *Wings*
November 28 1975 UK
October 27 1975 USA #12

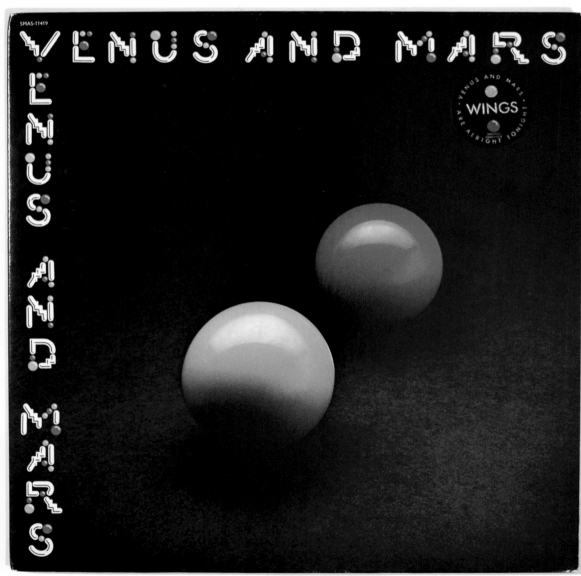

Wings at the Speed of Sound

by *Wings*

March 26 1976 UK #2
March 22 1976 USA #1

produced by Paul McCartney

Let 'Em In
The Note You Never Wrote
She's My Baby
Beware My Love
Wino Junko
Silly Love Songs
Cook of the House
Time to Hide
Must Do Something About It
San Ferry Anne
Warm and Beautiful

With a settled lineup, the cohesion cemented by months on the road was much in evidence on *Wings at the Speed of Sound*, where everyone had at least one lead vocal performance. The strong impression was stability, and the music wasn't bad either with two more hardy perennials emerging in *Let 'Em In* and *Silly Love Songs*. Four of the songs went into the Wings

Wings Over America
by *Wings*

December 10 1976 UK #8
December 10 1976 USA #1
produced by Paul McCartney

Over America tour, with which the album's release was meant to coincide. (As it happened, the tour was then delayed by a couple of months.)

Medley: Venus And Mars/Rock Show/Jet
Let Me Roll It
Spirits of Ancient Egypt
Medicine Jar
Maybe I'm Amazed
Call Me Back Again
Lady Madonna
The Long and Winding Road
Live and Let Die
Picasso's Last Words (Drink to Me)
Richard Cory
Bluebird
I've Just Seen A Face
Blackbird
Yesterday
You Gave Me the Answer
Magneto and Titanium Man
Go Now
My Love
Listen to What the Man Said
Let 'Em In
Time to Hide
Silly Love Songs
Beware My Love
Letting Go
Band on the Run
Hi, Hi, Hi
Soily

Maybe I'm Amazed

Words and Music by PAUL McCARTNEY

Recorded by WINGS on Capitol Records

Singles
Maybe I'm Amazed /Soily by *Wings*
February 4 1977 UK #28
February 7 1977 USA #10

Selected from ninety hours of recordings, *Wings Over America* is
a faithful account of the 1975–76
world tour, taped at several of
the US shows (but mixed as if it
were a single performance). Though
an expensive triple-disc, sales
were remarkable – it remains one of
very few live albums to make number one in America. Wings at their
concerted zenith.

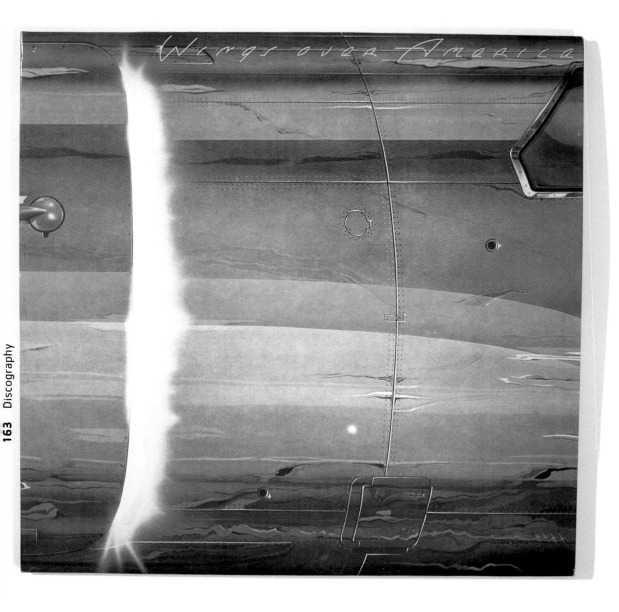

London Town
by *Wings*

March 31 1978 UK #4
March 27 1978 USA #2

produced by Paul McCartney

London Town
Cafe On The Left Bank
I'm Carrying
Backwards Traveller
Cuff Link
Children Children
Girlfriend
I've Had Enough
With A Little Luck
Famous Groupies
Deliver Your Children
Name and Address
Don't Let It Bring you Down
Morse Moose and the Grey Goose

Paul and Linda's zeal for recording in exotic locale was perpetuated with *London Town*. Though the album was started and finished in that city (at Abbey Road, where Wings did most of their work), sessions also took place on a boat moored off the us Virgin Islands, and in the barn attached to Paul and Linda's remote Scottish farm. A melodic and interesting collection, it nonetheless caught Wings mid-transition once more, with Jimmy and Joe leaving after its start but before its completion. Their absence from the cover artwork was emphatic confirmation that Wings were now a threesome once again.

I've Had Enough /
Deliver Your Children by *Wings*

June 16 1978 UK #42
June 5 1978 USA #25

Singles
Mull of Kintyre / Girls' School by *Wings*

November 11 1977 UK #1
November 14 1977 USA #33
Girls' School was the preferred A-side in America, and it was this which made #33

London Town / I'm Carrying by *Wings*

August 11 1978 UK #60
August 14 1978 USA #39

With a Little Luck /
Backwards Traveller—Cuff Link

by *Wings*
March 24 1978 UK #5
March 20 1978 USA #1

Goodnight Tonight /
Daytime Nightime Suffering by *Wings*

March 23 1979 UK #5
March 19 1979 USA #5
Goodnight Tonight also issued in extended 'Long Version'

Back to the Egg *by Wings*

June 8 1979 UK #6
June 11 1979 USA #8
produced by Paul McCartney & Chris Thomas

Reception
Getting Closer
We're Open Tonight
Spin It On

Again and Again and Again
Old Siam, Sir
Arrow Through Me
Rockestra Theme
To You
After the Ball / Million Miles
Winter Rose / Love Awake
The Broadcast
So Glad To See You Here
Baby's Request

STEREO EPS-81200

Back to the Egg was intended to signify a fresh beginning. With the addition of young but experienced musicians Steve Holly (drums) and Laurence Juber (guitar), Wings were back to being a five-piece and greater energy abounded, influenced by the advent of voguish new wave and the prospect of another inter-continental tour. But the law of sod has a devious scheme for 'best laid plans' ... The album was in fact Wings' swansong, and the planned tour was abruptly halted after the British leg thanks to the little matter of Paul's Tokyo incarceration. Recorded in a castle in Kent, south-east England, Back to the Egg hatched no real hits but is enjoyed by many for its quirkiness.

Full circle. Ten years after McCartney came McCartney II, recorded in much the same way: Paul alone at home, microphone straight into tape machine. Though its making pre-dated Wings' abrupt bow – indeed the project was conceived for private consumption, not general release – the absence of any other musicians did not bode well for the future for Denny Laine and co. Listeners

Single
Wonderful Christmastime / Rudolph the Red-Nosed Reggae by *Paul McCartney*
November 16 1979 UK #6
November 26 1979 USA

McCartney II
by *Paul McCartney*

May 16 1980 UK #1   May 26 1980 USA #3
produced by Paul McCartney

Coming Up
Temporary Secretary
On the Way
Waterfalls
Nobody Knows
Front Parlour
Summer's Day Song
Frozen Jap
Bogey Music
Darkroom
One of These Days

heard a stripped-down sound and much in the way of musical experimentation – standout tracks *Coming Up,* a disco hit, and the highly melodic *Waterfalls* were unrepresentative of their fellow travellers. A number one in the summer of 1980.

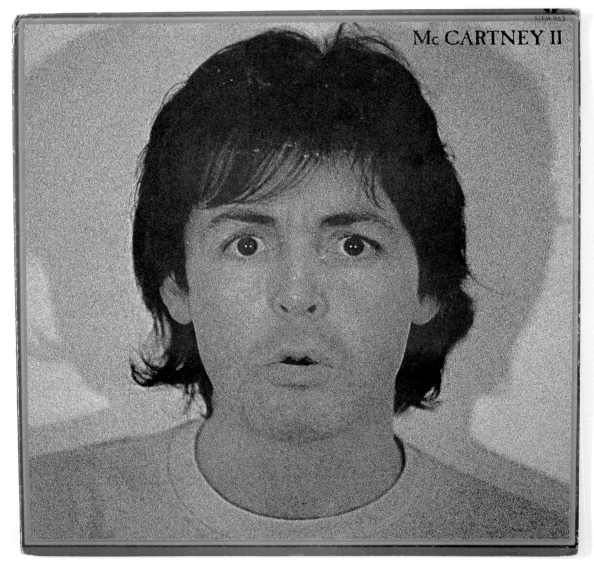

Mc CARTNEY II

SLEM-963

Singles

Coming Up by *Paul McCartney* / **Coming Up (Live at Glasgow)** / **Lunch Box / Odd Sox**

by *Paul McCartney & Wings*
April 11 1980 UK #2
April 14 1980 USA #1
The live version of Coming Up was the preferred version in America, and it was this which made #1

Waterfalls / Check My Machine

by *Paul McCartney*
June 13 1980 UK #9
July 22 1980 USA

Temporary Secretary / Secret Friend by *Paul McCartney*

September 12 1980 UK

Thrillington

orchestral version of *Ram*, released under pseudonym *Percy "Thrills" Thrillington*

April 29 1977 UK
May 16 1977 USA

Too Many People
3 Legs
Ram On
Dear Boy
Uncle Albert / Admiral Halsey
Smile Away
Heart of the Country
Monkberry Moon Delight
Eat at Home
Long Haired Lady
The Back Seat of My Car

Wings Greatest

hits compilation

December 1 1978 UK #2
November 27 1978 USA #29

Another Day
Silly Love Songs
Live and Let Die

Junior's Farm
With a Little Luck
Band on the Run
Uncle Albert / Admiral Halsey
Hi Hi Hi
Let 'Em In
My Love
Jet
Mull of Kintyre

Concerts for the People of Kampuchea

by various artists
(including *Paul McCartney & Wings*)

April 6 1981 UK #39
March 30 1981 USA #36

produced by Chris Thomas (recorded live at Hammersmith Odeon, December 29 1979)

Got to Get You Into My Life
Every Night
Coming Up
Lucille
Let It Be
Rockestra Theme

other albums of note:

McGear, a 1974 album by Mike McGear, produced by (his brother) Paul McCartney, and featuring Wings. Paul wrote or co-wrote several of the songs.

Holly Days, 1977 album by Denny Laine featuring cover versions of ten Buddy Holly songs. The instruments were played by Paul McCartney, who also sang backing vocals and produced; Linda also contributed vocals. A Wings album in all but name.

Wide Prairie, Linda McCartney's album, issued posthumously in 1998, contained several previously unreleased 1970s recordings – the title track, *New Orleans*, *I Got Up*, *Mister Sandman*, *Oriental Nightfish* and *Sugartime*, as well as the previously issued *Seaside Woman*, *B-Side To Seaside* and *Cook Of The House*.

Wrapping it up

other singles:

Walking In The Park With Eloise / Bridge Over The River Suite

October 18 1974 UK
December 2 1974 USA

released under pseudonym *The Country Hams*

Uncle Albert /Admiral Halsey / Eat at Home

April 22 1977 UK

released under pseudonym *Percy "Thrills" Thrillington*

Seaside Woman /B–Side To Seaside
Seaside Woman /B–Side To Seaside

May 31 1977 UK #59

Linda McCartney with *Wings*, released under pseudonym *Suzy and the Red Stripes*

released as a single in the UK on August 10 1979, July 18 1980 and July 7 1986

and

Mama's Little Girl, a previously unissued Wings track from 1972, was issued in 1990 and is included on the currently available *Wild Life* CD as a bonus track.

My Carnival, a previously unissued Wings track from 1975, was issued in 1985 and is included on the currently available *Venus and Mars* CD as a bonus track.

Wingspan – Hits and History

May 7 2001 UK #5
May 8 2001 USA #2

Listen to What the Man Said
Band on the Run
Another Day
Live and Let Die
Jet
My Love
Silly Love Songs
Pipes of Peace
C Moon
Hi Hi Hi
Let 'Em In
Goodnight Tonight
Junior's Farm
Mull of Kintyre
Uncle Albert /Admiral Halsey
With A Little Luck
*Coming Up
No More Lonely Nights

Let Me Roll It
The Lovely Linda
Daytime Nightime Suffering
Maybe I'm Amazed
Helen Wheels
Bluebird
Heart of the Country
Every Night
Take It Away
Junk
Man We Was Lonely
Medley: Venus and Mars /Rock Show
The Back Seat of My Car
Rockestra Theme
Girlfriend
Waterfalls
Tomorrow
Too Many People
Call Me Back Again
Tug Of War
Medley: Bip Bop /Hey Diddle
No More Lonely Nights Playout Version

*The UK album featured the Paul McCartney recording, the US album substituted Wings' live version.

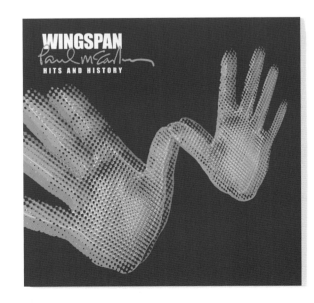

1972

British universities

February 9	Nottingham
February 10	York
February 11	Hull
February 13	Newcastle-upon-Tyne
February 14	Lancaster
February 16	Town Hall, Leeds
February 17	Sheffield
February 18	Salford
February 21	Birmingham
February 22	Swansea
February 23	Oxford

European tour

July 9	Centre Culturel, Chateau Vallon, near Toulon FRANCE
July 12	Théâtre Antique, Juan Les Pins FRANCE
July 13	Théâtre Antique, Arles FRANCE
July 16	Olympia Theatre, Paris FRANCE
July 18	Cirkus-Krone-Bau, Munich WEST GERMANY
July 19	Offenbach Halle, Frankfurt WEST GERMANY
July 21	Kongresshaus, Zurich SWITZERLAND
July 22	Pavilion, Montreux SWITZERLAND
August 1	K.B. Hallen, Copenhagen DENMARK
August 4	Messuhalli, Helsinki FINLAND
August 5	Kupittaan Urheiluhalli, Turku FINLAND
August 7	Kungliga Tennishallen, Stockholm SWEDEN
August 8	Idretshalle, Örebro SWEDEN
August 9	Njårdhallen, Oslo NORWAY
August 10	Scandinavium Halle, Gothenberg SWEDEN
August 11	Olympean, Lund SWEDEN
August 12	Fyns Forum, Odense DENMARK
August 14	Vejlby Risskov Hallen, Århus DENMARK
August 16	Rhinehalle, Düsseldorf WEST GERMANY
August 17	De Doelen, Rotterdam THE NETHERLANDS
August 19	Evenementenhal, Groningen THE NETHERLANDS
August 20	Concertgebouw, Amsterdam THE NETHERLANDS
August 21	Congresgebouw, The Hague THE NETHERLANDS
August 22	Ciné Roma, Antwerp BELGIUM
August 24	Deutschlandhalle, West Berlin WEST GERMANY

1973

March 18	Hard Rock Café, London (Release charity benefit)

British tour

May 11	Hippodrome, Bristol
May 12	New Theatre, Oxford
May 13	Capitol Cinema, Cardiff
May 15	Winter Gardens, Bournemouth
May 16	Hard Rock, Manchester
May 17	Hard Rock, Manchester
May 18	Empire Theatre, Liverpool
May 19	Leeds University
May 21	Guildhall, Preston
May 22	Odeon Cinema, Newcastle-upon-Tyne
May 23	Odeon Cinema, Edinburgh
May 24	Green's Playhouse, Glasgow
May 25	Odeon Cinema, Hammersmith
May 26	Odeon Cinema, Hammersmith
May 27	Odeon Cinema, Hammersmith
July 4	City Hall, Sheffield
July 6	Odeon Cinema, Birmingham
July 9	Odeon Cinema, Leicester
July 10	City Hall, Newcastle-upon-Tyne

1975

British tour

September 6	Elstree Film Studios (warm-up)
September 9	Gaumont Cinema, Southampton
September 10	Hippodrome, Bristol
September 11	Capitol Cinema, Cardiff
September 12	Free Trade Hall, Manchester
September 13	Hippodrome, Birmingham
September 15	Empire Theatre, Liverpool
September 16	City Hall, Newcastle-upon-Tyne
September 17	Odeon Cinema, Hammersmith
September 18	Odeon Cinema, Hammersmith
September 20	Usher Hall, Edinburgh
September 21	Apollo Theatre, Glasgow
September 22	Capitol Cinema, Aberdeen
September 23	Caird Hall, Dundee

Australian tour

November 1	Entertainment Centre, Perth
November 4	Apollo Stadium, Adelaide
November 5	Apollo Stadium, Adelaide
November 7	Horden Pavilion, Sydney
November 8	Horden Pavilion, Sydney
November 10	Festival Hall, Brisbane
November 11	Festival Hall, Brisbane
November 13	Myer Music Bowl, Melbourne
November 14	Myer Music Bowl, Melbourne

Wings stage

1976

European tour

March 20	Falkoner Theatre, Copenhagen DENMARK
March 21	Falkoner Theatre, Copenhagen DENMARK
March 23	Deutschlandhalle, West Berlin WEST GERMANY
March 25	Ahoy Sportpaleis, Rotterdam THE NETHERLANDS
March 26	Pavilion, Paris FRANCE

Wings Over America

May 3	Tarrant County Convention Center, Fort Worth
May 4	The Summit, Houston
May 7	Olympia Stadium, Detroit
May 8	Olympia Stadium, Detroit
May 9	Maple Leaf Gardens, Toronto CANADA
May 10	Richfield Coliseum, Richfield
May 12	The Spectrum, Philadelphia
May 14	The Spectrum, Philadelphia
May 15	Capitol Centre, Washington DC
May 16	Capitol Centre, Washington DC
May 18	Omni Coliseum, Atlanta
May 19	Omni Coliseum, Atlanta
May 21	Nassau Coliseum, Long Island
May 22	Boston Garden, Boston
May 24	Madison Square Garden, New York
May 25	Madison Square Garden, New York
May 27	Riverfront Coliseum, Cincinnati
May 29	Kemper Arena, Kansas City
May 31	Chicago Stadium, Chicago
June 1	Chicago Stadium, Chicago
June 2	Chicago Stadium, Chicago
June 4	Civic Center, St Paul
June 7	McNichols Sports Arena, Denver
June 10	Kingdome, Seattle
June 13	Cow Palace, San Francisco
June 14	Cow Palace, San Francisco
June 16	Sports Arena, San Diego
June 18	Community Center Music Hall, Tucson
June 21	Forum, Los Angeles
June 22	Forum, Los Angeles
June 23	Forum, Los Angeles

European tour

September 19	Stadthalle, Vienna AUSTRIA
September 21	Dome Sportova Hall, Zagreb YUGOSLAVIA
September 25	St Mark's Square, Venice ITALY (UNESCO/Venice in Peril)
September 27	Olympiahalle, Munich WEST GERMANY

Conclusion of tour ENGLAND

October 19	Empire Pool, Wembley
October 20	Empire Pool, Wembley
October 21	Empire Pool, Wembley

1979

British tour

November 23	Royal Court Theatre, Liverpool (warm-up)
November 24	Royal Court Theatre, Liverpool
November 25	Royal Court Theatre, Liverpool
November 26	Royal Court Theatre, Liverpool
November 28	Apollo Theatre, Ardwick, Manchester
November 29	Apollo Theatre, Ardwick, Manchester
December 1	Gaumont Cinema, Southampton
December 2	Brighton Centre, Brighton
December 3	Odeon Cinema, Lewisham
December 5	Rainbow Theatre, Finsbury Park
December 7	Empire Pool, Wembley
December 8	Empire Pool, Wembley
December 9	Empire Pool, Wembley
December 10	Empire Pool, Wembley
December 12	Odeon Cinema, Birmingham
December 14	City Hall, Newcastle-upon-Tyne
December 15	Odeon Cinema, Edinburgh
December 16	Apollo Theatre, Glasgow
December 17	Apollo Theatre, Glasgow
December 29	Odeon Cinema, Hammersmith (UNICEF)

1980

Japanese tour

JAPANESE TOUR CANCELLED

January 21	Nippon Budokan Hall, Tokyo
January 22	Nippon Budokan Hall, Tokyo
January 23	Nippon Budokan Hall, Tokyo
January 24	Nippon Budokan Hall, Tokyo
January 25	Aichi-ken Taiiku-kan, Nagoya
January 26	Aichi-ken Taiiku-kan, Nagoya
January 28	Osaka Furitsu Taiiku-kan, Osaka
January 29	Osaka Furitsu Taiiku-kan, Osaka
January 31	Nippon Budokan Hall, Tokyo
February 1	Nippon Budokan Hall, Tokyo
February 2	Nippon Budokan Hall, Tokyo

Index

NO. 1. 1974 **wings** P.O. Box 4UP
LONDON W1A 4UP.

McCartney No.6
PO Box 4UP
London W1a 4UP

PO Box 4UP **Wings** No.
London W1A 4UP

This newsletter is to make up for the one you missed out
on a few months ago. . . . sorry its a bit late, but at the
time there really wasn't much news. Before Paul and Linda
left for Lagos to record Band on the Run they did lots of
interviews. The following article appeared in Lucky Rider
a horsey mag.

Paul and Linda McCartney like so many popsters these days
retreat to the peace & quiet of the country whenever they
can.

Linda has loved horses since she was small and she started
taking lessons at a local stable when she was 9. "I was
instructed by a very good teacher, I always dreamed of hav
ing my own horse but my parents weren't struck on the idea."
Right from the start Linda showed a natural gift for riding.
As a child she competed in many horse shows and won lots of
ribbons and tropies. "I didn't jump though, I rode mainly in
equitation classes." Just about the biggest show venue she
attended was Madison Square Garden in New York. "It was a
great thrill, but I didn't win anything."

Apart from riding Linda says her other hobbies are
photography, music, cooking and life. But it was not till
she and Paul bought their farm in Scotland that she was at
last able to own the horse she'd always wanted. And not just
one horse either, but five. Two of which are ponies.

Lindas favorite horse is Cinnamon. She's a cheastnut mare,
and although well schooled, she's certainly got a mind of
her own. The first time she demonstrated this was the day
after Linda bought her "She was very nervous and didn't
fell at all at home. Paul and I went for a ride along an
idyllic river and decided to tie the horses up and sit in
the tall grass by the river, just like in the movies. However Cinnamon broke her reins and galloped off towards the
main road. I jumped on Paul's horse and rode after her. We
finally found her in someone's garden She jumped the fence

wings
Official Fun Club

SPECIAL U.K. TOUR ISSUE

November, 1975
P.O. Box 4UP
London W1A 4UP

Photographs

Linda McCartney *front cover bottom right, cover left flap top left and bottom left, cover right flap bottom right, 4, 8, 13–21, 24–28, 30 top, 31 top left and bottom left, 32 top, 53 left, 56–68, 72, 74–8, 79 right, 80 bottom right, 81, 127, 131, 132 left, 133–135, 138 bottom left*

Mike Berkofski *front cover top left, cover right flap bottom left 137*

Daily Mirror cover *22 courtesy of the Daily Mirror*

Chalkie Davis *136*

Henry Diltz *55, 120–6, 128, 129*

Robert Ellis *back cover bottom left, cover left flap bottom right, inside front and back covers, 6, 41, 42, 54 left, 82, 84, 85, 86 top left, 87–117, 149, 150*

Tommy Hanley *front cover bottom left, 52*

Graham Hughes *cover right flap top right, 130, 140*

Barry Lategan *32 bottom*

Linda McCartney archive *front cover top right, back cover top left and bottom right, 31 bottom right, 34, 36, 49, 51, 53 right*

Paul McCartney *11, 12, 118–119*

The Mainichi Newspaper *143*

Barry Morgan *80 top*

Philip Morris *71, 83*

MPL Archive *cover right flap top left, cover left flap top right, 23, 30, 35 right, 37, 38, 44, 47, 50, 54 bottom right, 69, 79 left, 80 bottom left*

Gerard Rada Nedich *1, 22, 86 bottom, 152–176*

Gene Nocon *138 right, 139 top left, bottom left, top right*

Rex Features *6*

Joseph Stevens *48*

David Thorpe *138 top left, 139 bottom centre, bottom right*

Mark Vigars *132 right, 133*

Photographs taken by Linda McCartney supplied by The Estate of Linda McCartney and MPL Communications Ltd / Inc

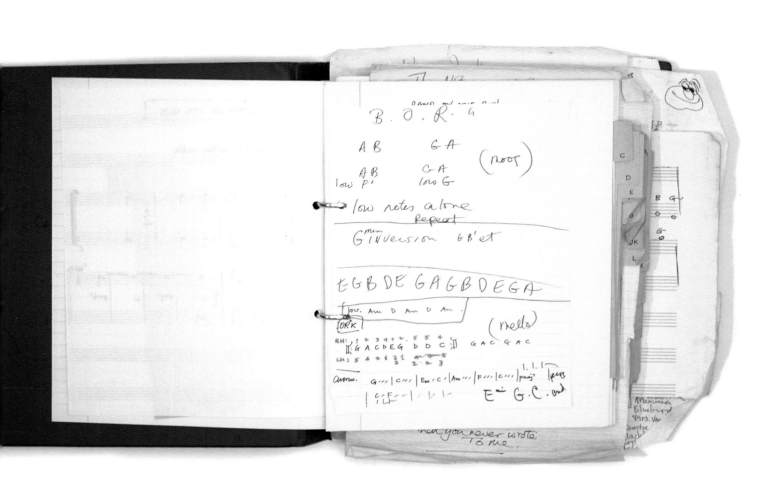